CW00735426

Reconceptualising Reflection in Reflective Practice

This edited volume presents a model that embraces four components of reflective practice: planning, acting, reflecting and evaluating. The complexities of reflective practice are manifested through three aspects of reflection: problem-solving, action-orientedness and critical reflection. To provide practical guidance, the audience is presented with various sets of experiences within the field of education which represent different foci and criticality of reflection. The experiences are described through different lenses, from individual to groups of educators.

The chapters provide a reconceptualisation of reflection which underpins an effective reflective practice. Therefore, readers are provided with information that demonstrates the different phases of reflection that make up an effective cycle of reflective practice. It is through the chapters that readers will be able to distinguish the different foci and levels of reflection, thus enabling them to engage in reflective practice more effectively.

The Malaysian context that the book brings gives readers insights into a lesser-known context and its people, culture, and educational system as a whole for comparison. The book is written with the needs of student teachers and teacher educators in mind. However, the model reconceptualised is transferable to other disciplines too.

Misrah Mohamed is Academic Developer at the University of West London, United Kingdom. She holds a PhD in Education from the University of Warwick, an MEd in Teaching English as a Second Language (TESL) from the National University of Malaysia and a BEd in TESL from the Universiti Putra Malaysia.

Radzuwan Ab Rashid is Associate Professor of Education and Discourse Studies at Universiti Sultan Zainal Abidin, Malaysia. He obtained his PhD in Education from the University of Nottingham, United Kingdom, and completed his postdoctoral fellowship at the University of Leeds exploring Applied Linguistics in an educational context.

Routledge Research in Education

This series aims to present the latest research from right across the field of education. It is not confined to any particular area or school of thought and seeks to provide coverage of a broad range of topics, theories and issues from around the world.

Plurilingual Pedagogy in the Arabian Peninsula
Transforming and Empowering Students and Teachers
Edited by Daniela Coelho and Telma Gharibian Steinhagen

Theoretical and Historical Evolutions of Self-Directed Learning
The Case for Learner-Led Education
Caleb Collier

Learning as Interactivity, Movement, Growth and Becoming, Volume 1
Ecologies of Learning in Higher Education
Edited by Mark E. King and Paul J. Thibault

The New Publicness of Education
Democratic Possibilities After the Critique of Neo-Liberalism
Edited by Carl Anders Säfström and Gert Biesta

New Directions in Rhizomatic Learning
From Poststructural Thinking to Nomadic Pedagogy
Edited by Myint Swe Khine

Reconceptualising Reflection in Reflective Practice
Voices from Malaysian Educators
Edited by Misrah Mohamed and Radzuwan Ab Rashid

For more information about this series, please visit: www.routledge.com/Routledge-Research-in-Education/book-series/SE0393

Reconceptualising Reflection in Reflective Practice

Voices from Malaysian Educators

Edited by Misrah Mohamed
and Radzuwan Ab Rashid

Routledge
Taylor & Francis Group

LONDON AND NEW YORK

First published 2023
by Routledge
4 Park Square, Milton Park, Abingdon, Oxon OX14 4RN

and by Routledge
605 Third Avenue, New York, NY 10158

*Routledge is an imprint of the Taylor & Francis Group, an
informa business*

© 2023 selection and editorial matter, Misrah Mohamed and
Radzuwan Ab Rashid; individual chapters, the contributors

The right of Misrah Mohamed and Radzuwan Ab Rashid to
be identified as the authors of the editorial material, and of
the authors for their individual chapters, has been asserted
in accordance with sections 77 and 78 of the Copyright,
Designs and Patents Act 1988.

British Library Cataloguing-in-Publication Data
A catalogue record for this book is available from the
British Library

ISBN: 978-1-032-44843-5 (hbk)
ISBN: 978-1-032-44846-6 (pbk)
ISBN: 978-1-003-37419-0 (ebk)

DOI: 10.4324/9781003374190

Typeset in Times New Roman
by Apex CoVantage, LLC

Contents

Contributors

Ab Rahman, Nur Afiqah is an Academic Skills Adviser at the University of Birmingham, UK. She qualifies as a Fellow of the Higher Education Academy (FHEA), UK. She has a PhD in Education from the University of Warwick. She previously worked as an English teacher and a lecturer in Malaysia. Her research interests include language learning, vocabulary learning, academic skills, academic writing and special education needs.

Ab Rashid, Radzuwan is an Associate Professor of Education and Discourse Studies at Universiti Sultan Zainal Abidin, Malaysia. He graduated from the University of Nottingham, UK (PhD in Education) and completed his postdoctoral fellowship at the University of Leeds, UK. He has published research articles in highly indexed journals and his books were published by the A-list publishers. In 2019, Clarivate Analytics (Web of Knowledge) nominated him for the Malaysia Research Star Award.

Azlan, Mohammad Affiq Kamarul is a Senior Language Teacher at the Centre for Language Studies and Generic Development, Universiti Malaysia Kelantan (UMK), Malaysia. He received his first degree majoring in TEFL and his master's degree in Applied Linguistics. Specialising in the teaching of English as a Second Language, he has been teaching at primary, secondary and tertiary levels. He is currently the e-learning coordinator for the English Language Department at UMK.

Khairuddin, Zurina is a Senior Lecturer at the Centre of English Language Studies, Faculty of Languages and Communication, Universiti Sultan Zainal Abidin (UniSZA), Malaysia. She graduated from the University of Auckland, New Zealand (BEd TESOL), Universiti Teknologi Mara, Malaysia (MEd TESL) and University of Sussex, UK (PhD in Linguistics). Her research interests are in the areas of applied linguistics, intercultural communication, identity and Teaching of English as a Second Language (TESL).

Mohamed, Misrah is an Academic Developer at the University of West London, UK. She graduated from the University of Warwick, UK (PhD in Education), the National University of Malaysia, Malaysia (MEd in TESL) and the Universiti Putra Malaysia, Malaysia (BEd in TESL). She has experienced teaching in the higher education institutions in Malaysia, Ireland and UK. She has published an award-winning workbook and authored scholarly articles nationally and internationally.

Mohd Nawi, Noor Syamimie serves as a Language Teacher of English Language Department in Universiti Malaysia Kelantan, Malaysia. She received her MD in Linguistics from University of Malaya (UM). Currently, she teaches English for Specific Purpose (ESP) courses on English for Science and English for Workplace.

Ramamurthy, Lena serves as a Senior Language Teacher of English Language Department in Universiti Malaysia Kelantan, Malaysia. She received her MD in Applied Linguistics from University Utara Malaysia (UUM). Currently, she teaches English for Specific Purpose (ESP) courses on English for Business Communication and English for Workplace.

Shafien, Syakirah serves as a Senior Language Teacher of English Language Department in Universiti Malaysia Kelantan, Malaysia. She received her MD in Applied Linguistics from University Utara Malaysia (UUM). Currently, she teaches English for Specific Purpose (ESP) courses on English for Business Communication and English for Workplace.

Shukor, Siti Shuhaida is a Senior Lecturer at the Department of English Language and Literature, Faculty of Languages and Communication, Universiti Pendidikan Sultan Idris (UPSI), Malaysia. She graduated from the University of Warwick, UK (PhD in Education), Universiti Putra Malaysia, Malaysia (MSc in TESL), and Universiti Teknologi Malaysia, Malaysia (BSc with TESL). Her main research and passion revolve around Computer Assisted Language Learning, Blended Learning, Cultural Historical Activity Theory, Social Media and Collaborative Writing in English language learning and context.

Tun, Nadia is a Language Teacher at the Faculty of General Studies and Advanced Education, Universiti Sultan Zainal Abidin (UniSZA), Malaysia. She graduated from Universiti Industri Selangor (UNISEL), Selangor, Malaysia (BEd TESL) and University of Sussex, United Kingdom (MA Education). Her interests are in the areas of education, particularly Teaching English as a Second Language (TESL) and teacher's cognition. She is also interested in applied linguistics mainly on intercultural communication and identity.

Zainal, Saiful Izwan is a Senior Lecturer at Universiti Sains Islam Malaysia, Malaysia. He graduated from the University of Warwick, UK (PhD), Macquarie University, Sydney (B.Ed. TESOL) and the University of Malaya, Malaysia (Master of Education). He has served as an English language teacher and a lecturer at different education sectors in Malaysia. His areas of interest are English Language Teaching, Teaching English to Speakers of Other Languages (TESOL), and education.

Zamri, Norazrin is currently a Lecturer at Akademi Pengajian Bahasa (APB) UiTM, Shah Alam, Malaysia. She has qualifications in TESOL (BEd, Victoria University of Wellington, New Zealand), ESL (MA, Universiti Malaya, Malaysia) and applied linguistics (PhD, University of Warwick, UK). Her research interests include discursive identity construction and online discourses. This includes exploring the constructions of various sociocultural linguistic identities in multimodal discourses that are significant in diverse pedagogical and social media settings.

Preface

This book is inclusive of seven chapters written by Malaysian educators who have experienced navigating education systems in various countries. Through reflective writing, this book presents a model that embraces four components of reflective practice: planning, acting, reflecting and evaluating, and three key aspects of reflection: problem-solving, action orientedness and critical reflection.

In Chapter 1, authors present an overview of the concepts of effective reflective practice and discuss the value of reflection that can help educators to develop professionally. Based on a discussion of key aspects of reflective practice, a revised model is introduced and from this model, a framework of reflection is proposed. This framework is unfolded as a continuum to address the complexities of reflections and reflective practice which is presented in each recount from Chapter 2 to Chapter 7.

Having an idea and turning this book into what it is now is as hard as it sounds. The experience is both internally challenging and rewarding. The editors would like to take this opportunity to acknowledge the help of all the people involved in this project and, more specifically, to the authors and reviewers who took part in the review process. Without their support, this book would not have become a reality.

First, our sincere gratitude goes to the chapter's authors who contributed their time and expertise to this book. Thank you for your perseverance. Keep striving to grow and help others grow. Next, to the reviewers, thank you for providing feedback regarding the improvement of quality, coherence and content presentation of chapters. We appreciate the time you spent to give us constructive criticism. Finally, to all those who have been a part of us getting there; the proofreaders, the T&F Commissioning Editor and production team, and our family who have always been there when we needed them throughout the journey. Thank you is an understatement, but we value and appreciate your involvement and all the help.

Misrah Mohamed
University of West London, UK
Radzuwan Ab Rashid
Universiti Sultan Zainal Abidin, Malaysia

Acronyms and Abbreviations

APB	*Akademi Pengajian Bahasa* (Language Learning Academy)
AT	Activity theory
BL	Blended learning
CAL	Centre for applied linguistics
CD	Compact disk
CHAT	Cultural historical activity theory
CPD	Continuing professional development
EAP	English for academic purposes
ESL	English as a second language
EU	European Union
F2f	Face-to-face
FL	Foreign language
HE	Higher education
HKOU	Hong Kong Open University
HOTS	Higher order thinking skills
ICT	Information and communications technology
IELTS	International English language testing system
IG	Instagram
L2	Second language
LMS	Learning management system
MoE	Ministry of Education
MQF	Malaysian Qualifying Framework
MTS	Malaysian Teacher Standard
NEP	National Education Philosophy
PISA	Programme for International Student Assessment
PhD	Doctor of Philosophy
SMK	*Sekolah Menengah Kebangsaan* (secondary school)
SOLO	Structured of the Observed Learning Outcome
TESOL	Teaching English to speakers of other languages
UiTM	*Universiti Teknologi MARA*
UMK	*Universiti Malaysia Kelantan*
UDL	Universal Design for Learning
UK	United Kingdom
WA	WhatsApp

1 Conceptualising the Complexity of Reflection for Effective Reflective Practice

Mohamed, Misrah and Ab Rashid, Radzuwan

Introduction

In the field of education, reflective practice has been recognised as an important aspect in continuing professional development. Through reflective practice, we can identify the factors, the consequences of and the assumptions that underlie our actions. Reflective practice helps us to identify not only our strengths and weaknesses but also specific learning needs to maintain our professional competence.

In higher education, reflective practice has become a dynamic, participatory and cyclical process (Ai et al., 2017) that contributes to educators' professional development and personal growth (Back et al., 2009; McAlpine et al., 2004; Davies, 2012; Marshall, 2019). Without routinely engaging in reflective practice, it is unlikely that educators will comprehend the effects of their motivations, expectations and experiences upon their practice (Lubbe & Botha, 2020). Thus, reflective practice becomes an important tool that helps educators to explore and articulate lived experiences, current experience and newly created knowledge (Osterman & Kottkamp, 2004). Reflective practice can also foster professional competence and enable professional judgement (Day, 1999). Educators are continually recommended to apply reflective practice in getting a better understanding of what they know and do as they develop their knowledge of practice (Loughran, 2002; Lubbe & Botha, 2020). In fact, reflective practice is now a prominent part of training for trainee teachers.

Despite the wide acceptance of the concept of reflective practice, the notion of 'reflection' in itself is still broad. Our review of literature reveals that reflection is a term that carries diverse meaning. For some, 'it simply means thinking about something' or 'just thinking' (e.g. Loughran, 2002, p. 33), whereas for others, it is a well-defined practice with very specific purpose, meaning and action (e.g. Dewey, 1933; Grimmett & Erickson, 1988; Loughran, 2002; Paterson & Chapman, 2013; Richardson, 1990; Schön, 1983; Spalding et al., 2002). We found many interesting interpretations made along this continuum, but we believe the most appealing that rings true for most people is

DOI: 10.4324/9781003374190-1

that reflection is useful and informing in the development and understanding of teaching and learning. This, however, is not enough to signify the characteristics of reflection. Consequently, many teachers find it hard to understand the concept and engage in reflective practice for their professional development (Jay & Johnson, 2002; Burt & Morgan, 2014; Bennett-Levy & Lee, 2014; Haarhoff et al., 2015; Marshall, 2019). It is evident that an inability to reflect may result in poor insight and performance in practice (Davies, 2012). Therefore, we must embrace reflective practice; have an understanding of its importance and be proficient at practising it so we can maintain our professional standards. If we can foster our understanding of the reflective practice, we not only can reap its benefits for our own learning, but also facilitate and maximise reflective skills within our students.

In this chapter, we aim to provide an overview of the concepts of effective reflective practice and present the value of reflective practice that can help teachers to professionally develop. First, we situate our conceptual understanding of reflective practice by discussing key issues surrounding reflection and reflective practice. Second, we present the key aspects of effective reflective practice. Finally, based on our discussion of key aspects of effective reflective practice, we introduce a revised model of reflective practice that may serve as a guide for educators to professionally develop. Although the model is but one approach, we believe it holds promise for others grappling as we are with efforts to encourage reflective practices among educators.

Key Issues in Reflective Practice

The concepts of 'reflection', 'reflective thought' and 'reflective thinking' have been discussed since 1904, when John Dewey claimed that an individual with good ethical values would treat professional actions as experimental and reflect upon their actions and consequences. Dewey defined reflection as the 'active, persistent, and careful consideration of any belief or supposed form of knowledge in the light of the grounds that support it and the further conclusions to which it tends' (Dewey, 1904, p. 10). His basic notion is that reflection is an active, deliberative cognitive process involving a sequence of interconnected ideas that include the underlying beliefs and knowledge of an individual.

Following Dewey's original work and its subsequent interpretation, four key thought-provoking issues are worthy of discussion: reflective thinking versus reflective action; time of reflection; reflection and problem solving; and critical reflection. The first concern is whether reflection is a process limited to thinking about action or also bound up in action (Grant & Zeichner, 1984; Noffke & Brennan, 1988; Hatton & Smith, 1995). There seems to be broad agreement that reflection is a form of thought process (McNamara, 1990; Ross, 1989; Sparks-Langer et al., 1991; Hatton & Smith, 1995) even though some do not lead to action. However, Dewey's first mention of 'reflective action' suggests that he was concerned with the implementation of solutions after thinking through problems. Therefore, reflective practice, in our view, is bound up with the constant, careful consideration of practice in the light of knowledge and beliefs. The complete cycle of reflection should then lead to clear, modified action and this needs to be distinguished from routine action derived from impulse, tradition or authority (Gore & Zeichner, 1991; Hatton & Smith, 1995; Noffke & Brennan, 1988).

The time frames within which reflection takes place needs to be addressed – relatively immediate and short term, or rather more extended and systematic. Schön (1983) holds that professionals should learn to frame and reframe the problems they often face and after trying out various interpretations, modify their actions as a result. He proposes 'reflection-in-action', which requires conscious thinking and modification, simultaneously reflecting and doing almost immediately. Similar to this concept is 'technical reflection', involving thinking about competencies or skills and their effectiveness and occurs almost immediately after an implementation and can then lead to changes in subsequent action (Cruickshank, 1985; Killen, 1989). While the notion of immediacy in reflective practice seems appropriate, some argue that the process should involve conscious detachment from an activity after a distinct period of contemplation (Boud et al., 1985; Buchmann, 1990). This is because reflection demands contemplating rational and moral practices in order to make reasoned judgements about better ways to act. Reflective practice often involves looking back at actions from a distance, after they have taken place (Gore & Zeichner, 1991; Schön, 1983; Smith & Lovat, 1991). While immediate and extended 'versions' of reflections are both recognised, we suppose no one is better than another. However, we believe that being able to think consciously about what is happening and respond instantaneously makes for a higher level of reflective competence.

The third issue identified from our literature review is whether reflection by its very nature is problem orientated (Adler, 1991; Calderhead, 1989). Reflection is widely agreed to be a thought process concerned with finding solutions to real problems (Adler, 1991; Calderhead, 1989; Choy & Oo, 2012; Hatton & Smith, 1995; Loughran, 2002). However, it is unclear whether solving problems is an inherent characteristic of reflection. For example, Schön's (1983) reflection-in-action involves thought processing simultaneously with a group event taking place, and reflection-on-action refers to a debriefing process after an event. Both aims to develop insights into what took place – the aims, the difficulties during the event or experience and better ways to act. While focusing on reacting to practical events, these practices do not often intend to find solutions to specific practical problems. Instead, reflective practitioners are invited to think about a new set of actions from if not wider, at least different perspectives.

The fourth issue in the literature revolves around 'critical reflection'. Very often critical reflection is concerned with how individuals consciously consider their actions from within wider historical, cultural and political beliefs when framing practical problems for which to seek solutions

(Gore & Zeichner, 1991; Choy & Oo, 2012; Hatton & Smith, 1995). It is a measure of a person's acceptance of a particular ideology, its assumptions and epistemology, when critical reflection is developed within reflective practice (McNamara, 1990; Hatton & Smith, 1995). It implies the individual locates any analysis of personal action within her/his wider socio-historical and political-cultural contexts (Hatton & Smith, 1995; Noffke & Brennan, 1988; Smith & Lovat, 1991). While this makes sense, critical reflection in the literature appears to loosely refer to an individual's constructive self-criticism of their actions to improve in future (Calderhead, 1989), not a consideration of personal actions with both moral and ethical criteria (Adler, 1991; Gore & Zeichner, 1991; Senge, 1990). Thus, we see a need to define critical reflection in line with the key characteristics of reflective practice.

Effective Reflective Practice

Reflecting on the issues discussed earlier, we conclude that for reflective practice to be effective, it requires three key aspects: problem-solving, critical reflection and action-orientation. However, these aspects of reflective practice have different levels of complexity and meaning.

Problem-solving

A problem is unlikely to be acted upon if it is not viewed as a problem. Thus, it is crucial to problematise things during reflection, to see concerns that require improvement. This is not a simple process as people's ability to perceive things as problems is related to their previous experiences. For example, a senior teacher with years of teaching experience and a rapport with the students s/he teaches will be immediately aware of students experiencing difficulties with current teaching strategies. However, a junior teacher whose experience is restricted to a three-month placement and who has met students only a few times will be less aware. The differences in experience also influence the way people interpret problems. For example, the senior teacher may believe his/her teaching strategy is at fault if half the students cannot complete the given tasks. A junior teacher with only two weeks teaching experience may deduce that the students were not interested in the topic, and that is why they cannot complete the tasks given. This example illustrates the range of ways a problem can be perceived and the advantages of developing the ability to frame and reframe a problem (Schön, 1983).

Framing and reframing a problem through reflection can influence the practice of subsequent actions (Loughran, 2002). In the example given earlier, the junior teacher attributes the problem to the students' attitude, which gives her/him little to no incentive to address the situation. This is an ineffective reflective practice because it has little impact on the problem. Thus, we believe that it is crucial for individuals to not only recognise problems but also to examine their practices (Loughran, 2002) through a different lens to their existing perspectives so solutions can be developed and acted upon. This requires critical reflection.

Critical Reflection

We believe it is the critical aspect of reflection that makes reflective practice effective and more complex, formulated by various scholars as different stages of reflection. Zeichner and Liston (1987) proposed three stages of reflection similar to those described by Van Manen (1977). They suggested the first stage was 'technical reflection' on how far the means to achieve certain end goals were effective, without criticism or modification. In the second stage, 'practical reflection', both the means and the ends are examined, with the assumptions compared to the actual outcomes. This level of reflection recognises that meanings are embedded in and negotiated through language, hence are not absolute. The final stage, 'critical reflection', combined with the previous two, considers both the moral and ethical criteria of the judgements about professional activity (Adler, 1991; Gore & Zeichner, 1991; Senge, 1990).

While the three stages above capture the complexity of reflection, individuals will only reach an effective level of reflection when they are able to be self-critical in their judgements and reasoning and can expand their thinking based on new evidence. This aligns with Ross' (1989) five stages of reflection (see Table 1.1). In her five stages of reflection, individuals do not arrive at the

Table 1.1 Five stages of reflections (Ross, 1989)

	The individual:
Stage 1	• has a simple view of the world • believes knowledge to be absolute • views authority as the source of knowledge
Stage 2	• acknowledges existence of different viewpoints • believes knowledge to be relative • sees varying positions between right or wrong, no absolutes • uses unsupported personal beliefs frequently as 'hard' evidence when making decisions • views truth as 'knowable' but not yet known
Stage 3	• perceives legitimate differences of viewpoint • begins to develop the ability to interpret evidence • uses unsupported personal belief and evidence in making decisions but is beginning to be able to differentiate between them • believes that knowledge is uncertain in some areas
Stage 4	• views knowledge as contextually based • develops views that an integrated perspective can be evaluated as more or less likely to be true • develops an initial ability to integrate evidence to develop a coherent point of view
Stage 5	• exhibits all the characteristics listed in Stage 4 • possesses the ability to make objective judgements based on reasoning and evidence • is able to modify judgements based on new evidence if necessary

level of critical reflection until they get to stages 4 and 5, which require them to contextualise their knowledge and integrate the new evidence before making any judgements or modification (Van Gyn, 1996).

Action-orientation

We believe it is important that any reflections should be acted upon. Looking at the types and stages of reflection discussed earlier, there is a clear indication that reflective practice is a cyclical process (Babaei & Abednia, 2016; Clarke, 2008; Kolb, 1984; Oo & Habók, 2020; Pollard et al., 2014; Ratminingsih et al., 2018; Richards & Lockhart, 2005; Taggart & Wilson, 2005). Richards and Lockhart (2005) suggest this cyclical process comprises planning, acting, observing and reflecting. This is further developed by Hulsman et al. (2009) who believe that the cyclical process involves not only action and observation but also analysis, presentation and feedback. In the education field, reflective practice is also considered cyclical (Clarke, 2008; Pollard et al., 2014; Kennedy-Clark et al., 2018) because educators plan, observe, evaluate and revise their teaching practice continuously (Pollard et al., 2014). This process can be done through a constant systematic self-evaluation cycle (Ratminingsih et al., 2018) which involves a written analysis or an open discussion with colleagues.

From the descriptions above, it seems that cyclical reflective practice entails identifying a problem, exploring its root cause, modifying action plans based on reasoning and evidence, executing and evaluating the new action and its results. Within this cyclical process, we consider action as a deliberate change is the key to effective reflective practice, especially in the field of education. Reflection that is action-oriented is an ongoing process which refers to how educators prepare and teach and the methods they employ. Educators move from one teaching stage to the next while gaining the knowledge through experience of the importance/relevance of the chosen methods in the classroom situation (Oo & Habók, 2020).

An Effective Reflective Practice Model

While reflection is an invisible cognitive process, it is not altogether intuitive (Betsch, 2008). Individuals, especially those lacking experience, may lack adequate intuition (Greenhalgh, 2002) and need guidance to achieve a certain level of reflection. With this in mind, we have created a cyclical process of reflective practice which captures the three key aspects of reflective practice discussed earlier. This model may help teachers having a range of experience enhance their competence through different focus and levels of reflection (see Figure 1.1).

The model illustrates the cyclical process with three stages: reflection, modification and action. At the reflection stage, a problem and the root of the

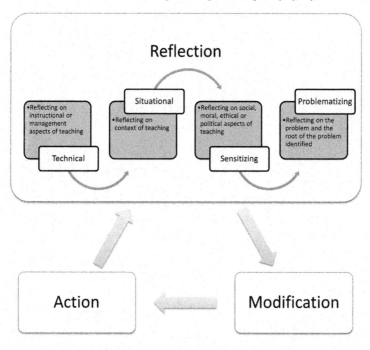

Figure 1.1 Cyclical reflective practice model capturing problem-solving, critical reflection and action-oriented

problem is explored so it can be framed as it is/was and then reframed to identify a possible solution. This is followed by a modification for change based on the reasoning and evidence explored during the reflection stage. Finally, the action stage involves executing action (an event), followed by the reflection stage to begin another cycle and continue the process.

The model above expands Tsangaridou and O'Sullivan's (1994) framework and highlights the four focuses of reflection; *technical* addresses the management or procedural aspects of teaching practice; *situational* addresses the context of teaching; *sensitising* involves reflecting upon the social, moral, ethical or political concerns of teaching; and *problematising* concerns the framing and reframing of the problem identified within the teaching context. Considering the different levels of critical reflection, we extend the four focuses of reflection to three different levels of critical reflection: descriptive involves reflection of the four focuses without reasoning or criticism; descriptive with rationale involves reflection of the four focuses with reasoning; and descriptive with rationale and evaluation involves reflection of the four focuses with both reasoning and criticism (see Table 1.2). Each of these

Table 1.2 A framework of reflection

Focus level	Technical	Situational	Sensitising	Problematising
1. Descriptive	Reflecting on the implementation of teaching by providing descriptive information about an action	Reflecting on the contextual aspects of teaching by providing descriptive information about the environment or situation	Reflecting on any other aspects of teaching by providing descriptive information about social, moral, ethical or political values that underpin an action	Reflecting on areas for development by providing descriptive information about the problem identified
2. Descriptive with rationale	Reflecting on the implementation of teaching by providing descriptive information about an action, and the rationale for an action (why it was carried out)	Reflecting on contextual aspects of teaching by providing descriptive information about the environment or situation, and the rationale for an action (why it was used in that specific context	Reflecting any other aspects of teaching by providing descriptive information about social, moral, ethical or political values that underpin an action, and the rationale for an action (concerning either the context or methods used, why decisions were made)	Reflecting on areas for development by providing descriptive information about the problem identified and its root (why the problem occurred)
3. Descriptive with rationale and evaluation	Reflecting on the implementation of teaching by providing descriptive information about an action, the rationale for an action, and evaluation of an action	Reflecting on contextual aspects of teaching by providing descriptive information about the environment or situation, rationale for an action (why it was used in that specific context, and evaluation of an action	Reflecting on social, moral, ethical or political aspects of teaching by providing descriptive information about social, moral, ethical or political values that underpin an action, and the rationale for an action (concerning either the context or methods used, why decisions were made), and evaluation of implications of an action	Reflecting on areas for development by providing descriptive information about the problem identified and its root (why the problem occurred) and evaluation of the logic underpinning the procedure (reframing problem)

levels requires different degrees of critical analysis and competence to extract information from actions and experiences. Overall, level three best captures effective critical reflection for each focus. This revised model that we proposed encompasses different levels of critical reflection and is action-oriented. There is also a clear link to problem-solving which requires framing and reframing problems to accurately identify them, which may influence the value and effectiveness of the actions that follow (Loughran, 2002). Thus, this model may help people to recognise the different aspects of reflection so they can make better assessments of and modifications to their procedures (Ross, 1989; Van Gyn, 1996).

Conclusion

The meaning of reflection and reflective practice is not clear cut. However, we believe a reflective educator should cultivate a set of responses to how their teaching operates in practice. As Dewey (1933) suggested, educators must find time to reflect on their activity, knowledge and experience so that they can develop and more effectively serve their community, nurturing each student's learning. However, this does not always happen. Some educators do not reflect on their own practice because they find the concept of reflective practice difficult to put into practice for their professional development (Jay & Johnson, 2002; Burt & Morgan, 2014; Bennett-Levy & Lee, 2014; Haarhoff et al., 2015; Marshall, 2019).

Our review of the literature indicates that reflective practice is a complex process and some scholars argue that it should involve active thinking that is more bound up with action (Grant & Zeichner, 1984; Noffke & Brennan, 1988; Hatton & Smith, 1995). Thus, the complete cycle of reflective practice needs to be distinguished from routine action which may stem from impulse, tradition or authority (Gore & Zeichner, 1991; Hatton & Smith, 1995; Noffke & Brennan, 1988). In addition, some also argue that reflective practice involves the conscious detachment from an activity followed by deliberation (Boud et al., 1985; Buchmann, 1990), and therefore reflective practice should not occur immediately after action. Although this is acceptable, we believe that instant reflection and modification for future action can be a good indicator of an individual's level of reflective competence.

Reflective practice is an active process that requires individuals to make the tacit explicit. Thus, it is crucial to acknowledge that reflection is, by its very nature, problem-centred (Adler, 1991; Calderhead, 1989; Hatton & Smith, 1995; Loughran, 2002; Choy & Oo, 2012). Only with this in mind can individuals frame and reframe their actions or experiences to discover specific solutions. Reflective practice is also complex, requiring critical appraisal and consideration of various aspects of thought processes. Individuals must play close attention to what they do, evaluate what works and what does not work on a personal, practical and professional level (Gore & Zeichner, 1991; Hatton

& Smith, 1995; Choy & Oo, 2012). However, some would consider critical reflection as no more than constructive self-criticism of one's actions with a view to improve (Calderhead, 1989). Consequently, scholars have taken different approaches to reflective practice in teaching areas that include critical thinking (e.g. Loughran, 2002; Ross, 1989; Tsangaridou & O'Sullivan, 1994). These approaches had four components in common: reflecting (observing actions, reviewing, recollecting), planning for future action (thinking and considering), acting (practice, experience and learning) and evaluating (interpreting and assessing outcomes). We propose a model that embraces these four sub-areas and three key aspects of reflection: problem-solving, action orientation and critical reflection. We align these key aspects with level of criticality in a framework with detailed descriptors.

In attempting to initiate a productive dialogue between the stages of reflection and levels of criticality, this book stretches the framework proposed as a continuum from technical aspects to distinguish different aspects of critical reflection. Thus, each of the following chapters concerns two or more topics and aspects of critical reflection. It is hoped that the differences found in each demonstrate the complexities of reflection, while encouraging those struggling to adopt reflective practice which suits their needs.

Chapter 2 captures how the author reflects and constructs her pedagogical identities that are related to teaching positions, qualifications and other demographical aspects. In this chapter, all four focuses of reflection are present, and the author assimilates all levels of critical reflection. This is done through her attempt to evaluate and criticise the underlying negotiations of identities within and among academics, and make the case for educators to reflect upon and modify their teaching experiences and identities over time to better inform their current and future teaching and learning decisions.

Chapter 3 captures how the author unravels the formation and development of teacher cognition. The author focuses on the *situational* aspect by reflecting on his personal experience from the early years of his schooling up to when he is employed as a senior lecturer at a higher education institution. Through *problematising* and *sensitising*, he managed to make modifications to his actions and practice, which subsequently changes his teacher cognition.

Chapter 4 captures an insider-outsider perspective from an author about the opportunities and challenges faced in teaching in a country that has a different learning landscape from her home country. She draws upon what she has learned about the similarities and differences in regard to pedagogy, culture and professional development in the education system in the countries discussed. In this chapter, the author demonstrates the application of *technical* and *situational* aspects of her experience. She applies *sensitising* by reflecting on social, moral and ethical aspects that relate to her context. She identifies the challenges she faced adapting to the culture and new context and this aspect of *problematising* becomes the foundation of her reflection.

Chapter 5 presents an expression by the authors who believe that success to a curriculum reform is deeply rooted in teachers' perceptions and behaviours towards teaching and learning. They revisit their own beliefs by reflecting on their experiences as consumers and providers of education. In this chapter, the authors reflect majorly on the *technical* and *situational* aspects of education in Malaysia. *Problematising* and *sensitising* appear a little bit later in the chapter, where modifications are outlined as part of the product of their reflection.

Chapter 6 captures a full cycle of a reflective practice. The author presents a few sets of reflections (which encompasses all aspects and levels of reflection) in addressing her inquiries on the blended learning take up in language teaching. Through five elements of CHAT, she discovers the key to successful blended learning which lies within the access to technology, teachers' readiness and commitment, and support provided by the institution.

Chapter 7 presents authors' reflection of experiences in dealing with e-Campus, a Moodle-based learning management system (LMS) in the institution that they worked with. They describe the origin of e-Campus and provide a reflection on its implementation as well as the initiatives taken by the institution in encouraging users to use the system. This chapter demonstrates how the authors assimilate all the aspects and levels of reflection. They also describe the modification and action stages which appear in the reflective practice model. This is another chapter that has a clear presentation of the full cycle of a reflective practice.

Acknowledgement: The content in this chapter is an expansion of a conceptual analysis which was originally published in the *Frontiers in Psychology*, section Educational Psychology.

References

Adler, S. (1991). The reflective practitioner and the curriculum of teacher education. *Journal of Education for Teaching, 17*(2), 139–150.

Ai, A., Al-Shamrani, S., & Almufti, A. (2017). Secondary school science teachers' views about their reflective practices. *Journal of Teacher Education for Sustainability, 19*(1), 43–53. https://doi.org/10.1515/jtes-2017-0003

Babaei, M., & Abednia, A. (2016). Reflective teaching and self-efficacy beliefs: Exploring relationships in the context of teaching EFL in Iran. *Australian Journal of Teacher Education, 41*(9), 1–27. https://doi.org/10.14221/ajte.2016v41n9.1

Back, J., De Geest, E., Hirst, C., & Joubert, M. (2009). *Final report: Researching effective CPD in mathematics education (RECME)*. NCETM.

Bennett-Levy, J., & Lee, N. K. (2014). Self-practice and self-reflection in cognitive behaviour therapy training: What factors influence trainees' engagement and experience of benefit? *Behavioural and Cognitive Psychotherapy, 42*(1), 48–64.

Betsch, T. (2008). The nature of intuition and its neglect in research on judgment and decision making. *Intuition in Judgment and Decision Making*, 3–22.

Boud, D., Keogh, M., & Walker, D. (1985). *Reflection. Turning experience into learning*. Kogan Page.

Buchmann, M. (1990). Beyond the lonely, choosing will: Professional development in teacher thinking. *Teachers College Record, 91*, 482–508.

Burt, E., & Morgan, P. (2014). Barriers to systematic reflective practice as perceived by UKCC Level 1 and Level 2 qualified Rugby Union coaches. *Reflective Practice, 15*(4), 468–480.

Calderhead, J. (1989). Reflective teaching and teacher education. *Teaching and Teacher Education, 5*, 43–51.

Choy, S. C., & Oo, P. S. (2012). Reflective thinking and teaching practices: A precursor for incorporating critical thinking into the classroom? *Online Submission, 5*(1), 167–182.

Clarke, P. A. (2008). Reflective teaching model: A tool for motivation, collaboration, self- reflection, and innovation in learning. *Georgia Educational Research Journal, 5*(4), 1–18.

Cruickshank, D. (1985). Uses and benefits of reflective teaching. *Phi Delta Kappan, 66*(10), 704–706.

Davies, S. (2012). Embracing reflective practice. *Education for Primary Care, 23*(1), 9–12.

Day, C. (1999). Researching teaching through reflective practice. In J. J. Loughran (Ed.), *Researching teaching: Methodologies and practices for understanding pedagogy*. Falmer.

Dewey, J. (1904). The relation of theory to practice in education. In C. S. McMurray (Ed.), *Third yearbook of the national society for the scientific study of education* (pp. 9–30). University of Chicago Press.

Dewey, J. (1933). *How we think: A restatement of the relation of reflective thinking to the educative process*. D.C. Heath and Company

Gore, J., & Zeichner, K. (1991). Action research and reflective teaching in preservice teacher education: A case study from the United States. *Teaching and Teacher Education, 7*, 119–136.

Grant, C., & Zeichner, K. (1984). On becoming a reflective teacher. In C. Grant (Ed.), *Preparing for reflective teaching*. Allyn & Bacon.

Greenhalgh, T. (2002). Intuition and evidence – uneasy bedfellows? *British Journal of General Practice, 52*(478), 395–400.

Grimmett, P. P., & Erickson, G. L. (1988). *Reflection in teacher education*. Teachers College Press.

Haarhoff, B., Thwaites, R., & Bennett-Levy, J. (2015). Engagement with self-practice/self-reflection as a professional development activity: The role of therapist beliefs. *Australian Psychologist, 50*(5), 322–328.

Hatton, N., & Smith, D. (1995). Reflection in teacher education: Towards definition and implementation. *Teaching and Teacher Education, 11*(1), 33–49.

Hulsman, R. L., Harmsen, A. B., and Fabriek, M. (2009). Reflective teaching of medical communication skills with DiViDU: Assessing the level of student reflection on recorded consultations with simulated patients. *Patient education and counseling, 74*, 142–149. doi: 10.1016/j.pec.2008.10.009

Jay, J. K., & Johnson, K. L. (2002). Capturing complexity: A typology of reflective practice for teacher education. *Teaching and Teacher Education, 18*(1), 73–85.

Kennedy-Clark, S., Eddles-Hirsch, K., Francis, T., Cummins, G., Ferantino, L., Tichelaar, M., & Ruz, L. (2018). Developing pre-service teacher professional capabilities through action research. *Australian Journal of Teacher Education, 43*(9), 39–58. https://doi.org/10.14221/ajte.2018v43n9.3

Killen, L. (1989). Reflective teaching. *Journal of Teacher Education, 40*(2), 49–52.

Kolb, D. (1984). *Experiential learning: Experience as the source of learning and development*. Prentice Hall.

Loughran, J. J. (2002). Effective reflective practice: In search of meaning in learning about teaching. *Journal of Teacher Education, 53*(1), 33–43.

Lubbe, W., & Botha, C. S. (2020). The dimensions of reflective practice: A teacher educator's and nurse educator's perspective. *Reflective Practice, 21*(3), 287–300.

Marshall, T. (2019). The concept of reflection: A systematic review and thematic synthesis across professional contexts. *Reflective Practice, 20*(3), 396–415.

McAlpine, L., Weston, C., Berthiaume, D., Fairbank-Roch, G., & Owen, W. (2004). Reflection on teaching: Types and goals of reflection. *Educational Research and Evaluation, 10*(4–6), 337–363. https://doi.org/10.1080/1380361051233138 3489

McNamara, D. (1990). Research on teachers' thinking: Its contribution to educating student teachers to think critically. *Journal of Education for Teaching, 16*(2), 147–160.

Noffke, S., & Brennan, M. (1988). The dimensions of reflection: A conceptual and contextual analysis. *Paper presented at the annual meeting of the America Educational Research Association*, New Orleans.

Oo, T. Z., & Habók, A. (2020). The development of a reflective teaching model for reading comprehension in English language teaching. *International Electronic Journal of Elementary Education, 13*(1), 127–138.

Osterman, K. F., & Kottkamp, R. B. (2004). *Reflective practice for educators: Professional development to improve student learning.* Corwin Press.

Paterson, C., & Chapman, J. (2013). Enhancing skills of critical reflection to evidence learning in professional practice. *Physical Therapy in Sport, 14*(3), 133–138.

Pollard, A, Black-Hawkins, K., Hodges, G. C., Dudley, P., James, M., Linklater, H., Swaffield, S., Swann, M., Turner, F., Warwick, P., Winterbottom, M., & Wolpert, M. A. (2014). *Reflective teaching in schools* (4th ed.). Bloomsbury Publishing Plc.

Ratminingsih, N. M., Artini, L. P., & Padmadewi, N. N. (2018). Incorporating self and peer assessment in reflective teaching practices. *International Journal of Instruction, 10*(4), 165–184.

Richards, J. C., & Lockhart, C. (2005). *Reflective teaching in second language classrooms.* Cambridge University Press.

Richardson, V. (1990). The evolution of reflective teaching and teacher education. In M. Pugach (Ed.), *Encouraging reflective practice in education* (pp. 3–19). Teachers College Press.

Ross, D. D. (1989). First steps in developing a reflective approach. *Journal of Teacher Education, 40*(2), 22–30.

Schön, D. (1983). *The reflective practitioner: How professionals think in action.* Basic Books.

Senge, P. (1990). *The 5th discipline.* Doubleday.

Smith, D., & Lovat, T. (1991). *Curriculum: Action on reflection* (2nd ed.). Social Science Press.

Spalding, E., Wilson, A., & Mewborn, D. (2002). Demystifying reflection: A study of pedagogical strategies that encourage reflective journal writing. *Teachers College Record, 104*(7), 1393–1421.

Sparks-Langer, G., Colton, A., Pasch, M., & Starko, A. (1991). Promoting cognitive, critical, and narrative reflection. *Paper presented at the annual meeting of the American Educational Research Association*, Chicago, IL.

Taggart, G. L., & Wilson, A. P. (2005). *Becoming a reflective teacher. Promoting reflective thinking in teachers: 50 action strategies.* Corwin Press.

Tsangaridou, N., & O'Sullivan, M. (1994). Using pedagogical reflective strategies to enhance reflection among preservice physical education teachers. *Journal of Teaching in Physical Education, 14*(1), 13–33.

Van Gyn, G. H. (1996). Reflective practice: The needs of professions and the promise of cooperative education. *Journal of Cooperative Education, 31,* 103–131.

Van Manen, M. (1977). Linking ways of knowing with ways of being practical. *Curriculum Inquiry, 6*(3), 205–228.

Zeichner, K. M., & Liston, D. (1987). Teaching student teachers to reflect. *Harvard Educational Review, 57*(1), 23–48.

2 Discursive Negotiation of Pedagogical Identities across Diverse Settings

Zamri, Norazrin

Introduction

The following paragraph contains information about me as an educator and it is not misplaced. Its position in this chapter is to underscore the importance of profession-related identities – the ways educators perceive themselves and wish to be perceived in academia.

Norazrin Zamri (PhD) is currently a lecturer at Akademi Pengajian Bahasa (APB) Universiti Teknologi MARA (UiTM), Shah Alam, Malaysia. She has a Bachelor's, Master's, and Doctor of Philosophy (PhD) qualification in teaching English to speakers of other languages (TESOL) (Victoria University of Wellington, New Zealand), English as a second language (ESL) (Universiti Malaya, Kuala Lumpur) and Applied Linguistics (University of Warwick), respectively. Her main research interests include discursive identity construction as well as online discourses. More specifically, she is currently keen on exploring the constructions of various socio-cultural linguistic identities in multimodal discourses in diverse pedagogical and social media settings.

The biodata above is generally how I construct my sense of self and seek to be represented as an academician, particularly within the context of an academic book that I wish to publish in. In this chapter, I mainly reflect upon how I construct my pedagogical identities related to the labels attached to certain types of teaching positions, the interrelated qualifications as well as other demographical aspects. The discussion will extract reflections on my own teaching experience of around ten years as an English language educator in Malaysia, as well as in the United Kingdom, where I pursued my PhD study for about three and a half years. I am making a case for educators to reflect upon their teaching experiences and identities over time to better inform their current and future teaching and learning decisions as well as their wellbeing. This reflection also calls for researchers to be more self-reflexive, as an impartial study is impossible, so attempting is futile (Mann, 2016). This chapter

DOI: 10.4324/9781003374190-2

takes a reflexive stance by revealing my own pedagogic roles and their likely impact on the processes as well as the outcomes of my teaching and research endeavours over time.

Although scholarly discussions on the negotiation of pedagogical identities are relevant, this area is largely overlooked in the existing research – which almost always revolves around the identities of second language (L2) and foreign language (FL) learners and how these are connected to their motivation (Dörnyei & Ushioda, 2009; Phan, 2008). In the areas of discourse and identity and their relationship to teaching English in L2 and FL contexts, I accept the view that the identities of all those involved in an educational context are co-constructed. From an interpretivist paradigm and social constructionist perspective (Benwell & Stokoe, 2006; Bucholtz & Hall, 2005), I strongly believe that the identities of L2 learners are constructed and negotiated in relation to those of their educators. One person's identities cannot be examined separately from the other parties in the educational processes. Through critical reflections, I aim to turn the spotlight on such an overlooked research area to reveal the complex underlying identity negotiations within and between academicians, way beyond the clear-cut individual descriptions of an educator's identities as reflected in my biodata above.

Pedagogical Identities: A Brief Overview

Few scholars have attempted to define and identify pedagogical identities (Bernstein, 2000; Cambridge, 2010), which, arguably, are not very clear. As an educator and a discourse analyst, I define pedagogical identities as the identities constructed by educators in and through the daily discourses of teaching and learning – in agreement with Bernstein (2000) and Bucholtz and Hall (2005). Bernstein (2000), in particular, suggests that 'contrasting educational discourses construct contrasting retrospective, prospective, decentred (market) and decentred (therapeutic) pedagogic identities' (p. 199). Since I am narrating my reflections, the first two suggested time-related pedagogic identities are relevant in this chapter and will be referred to, where relevant.

Previous research on pedagogical identities mainly focused on professional identities. Wilson et al. (2013), for example, only explored the professional identities of medical officers in their research. Discussing professional identities in the teaching profession, perceived by many as professional in nature, is thus apparently inevitable (Alsup, 2008; Sachs, 2001). I, would like to suggest that an educator's sense of selves extends beyond his or her overt professional identities. Most previous scholarly work on identity construction uses 'identity' in the singular. Postmodern accounts see individuals as having identities – plural, multiple, complex, and most importantly, constituted through discourse (Benwell & Stokoe, 2010; Bucholtz & Hall, 2005; De Fina et al., 2006; Dörnyei & Ushioda,

2009). Also, every discourse is believed to be meaningful, ideological, and related to a variety of discourses (Benwell & Stokoe, 2010; Bucholtz & Hall, 2005). Therefore, I consistently use the plural forms 'identities and 'discourses' in this chapter. I will reflect on the ways I have constructed, negotiated, reinforced, challenged, resisted and redefined my pedagogical identities by occasionally referring to: (1) two core principles of identity construction processes, Bucholtz and Hall's (2005) *relationality* and *positionality* principles, and (2) two suggested identity positions in Bernstein's (2000) notion of pedagogic identity, *retrospective* and *prospective* pedagogical identities. These technical terms will be italicised when used in my reflections that follow.

A Chronological Account of My Teaching Experience

To help the reader follow my journey as an educator in the ensuing reflections, my teaching experiences since 2007 are summarised in Table 2.1. To summarise, my teaching experience began in 2007 as a trainee teacher for three months in a public secondary school in the last term of my undergraduate TESOL programme. I then became a part-time English language educator in a public university for one semester after my degree programme. A year later in 2009, I taught part-time in private colleges during my master's study before being hired as a full-time English language lecturer in a public university, which is also my current workplace. During my PhD unpaid leave in the United Kingdom, I was a one-off tutor for a few classes and workshops related to applied linguistics and research methodology to students at various tertiary levels (degree, masters and PhD) at my department in the University of Warwick, over the course of three years.

The following map of Malaysia (Figure 2.1) portrays the different states mentioned in Table 2.1 and in subsequent reflections.

Professional Labels and Identities

What does pedagogical identities mean? Most often, educators' professional identities are scrutinised, for example, Sachs (2001) points out, the construction of educators' professional identities influences pedagogical reforms due to the inextricable link between professional identities and activities. Professional identities are often discussed in relation to the many labels attached to different educators' positions. In Malaysia, these terms are important since its culture places great importance on using the correct form of address for specific positions (Abdullah, 2002). Each nation has underlying cultural values – hierarchy or egalitarianism, formality or informality (Lefringhausen et al., 2019). As a Malaysian, I can say that Malaysia prides itself on its preference for hierarchy and formality over freedom or casual behaviour, especially in formal settings. These values are reflected in the way the community

Table 2.1 Details of my teaching experiences

Time periods	Teaching positions	Educational institutions	Students' levels	Subjects taught
Three months in the second half of 2007	Trainee teacher on teaching practicum	A public secondary school, SMK (P_Sri Aman, Selangor, Malaysia	Form four secondary school students	English and literature
January–June 2008	Part-time (with full-time hours and salary) English language lecturer	A public university, Universiti Teknologi MARA (UiTM), Kedah, Malaysia	Undergraduate diploma students	English language proficiency courses
July–November 2009	Part-time (hourly-paid) English language lecturer	A private university, Taylor's University, Subang Jaya, Selangor, Malaysia	Foundation students	English language proficiency courses [including International English Language Testing System (IELTS)]
September–December 2009	Part-time (hourly-paid) English language lecturer	A private university, INTI University, Subang Jaya, Selangor, Malaysia	Undergraduate diploma international students	English language proficiency courses
June 2010–September 2015	Full-time English language lecturer (permanent position)	A public university, UiTM, Shah Alam, Selangor, Malaysia	Undergraduate diploma and degree students	English language proficiency courses
A few sessions within two terms in 2017	PhD student (associate tutor)	Centre for Applied Linguistics, The University of Warwick, UK	Masters' students	One-off research methods classes (e.g. NVivo, qualitative analysis and literature review)
Once within one term in 2017	PhD student (associate tutor)	Centre for Applied Linguistics, The University of Warwick, UK	PhD students	One-off research methods class (e.g. NVivo qualitative analysis)

A few sessions within two terms in 2018	PhD student (associate tutor)	Centre for Applied Linguistics, The University of Warwick, UK	Master's students	One-off research methods classes by the end of terms (e.g. qualitative analysis)
A few sessions within two terms in 2018	PhD student (associate tutor)	Centre for Applied Linguistics, The University of Warwick, UK	Undergraduate degree Hong Kong Open University (HKOU) students	Relevant subjects for Intercultural Pragmatics short course
A few sessions within two terms in 2019	PhD student (associate tutor)	Centre for Applied Linguistics, The University of Warwick, UK	Undergraduate degree HKOU students	Relevant subjects for Intercultural Pragmatics short course
A few sessions within two terms in 2019	PhD student (associate tutor)	Centre for Applied Linguistics, The University of Warwick, UK	Master's students	One-off research methods classes (e.g. qualitative analysis and writing research)
July 2019–now	Full-time English language senior* lecturer (permanent position)	A public university, UiTM, Shah Alam, Selangor, Malaysia	Degree students	English language proficiency and applied linguistics courses

Figure 2.1 Map of Malaysia ("Malaysia Map", 2019)

associates the use of correct forms of address with respect for others, especially for older people with higher qualification or with political standing, for example.

In Malaysia, the education settings of the educators greatly influence the 'kind' of educator s/he is – a 'teacher' or a '*cikgu*' if one is a schoolteacher. It is normal to call a teacher as 'teacher Aisyah' or '*Cikgu* Aisyah' – an example of collocating 'teacher' with the educator's first name, although it is also common for school educators to ask their students to use more generic salutations like '*Puan*' (Mrs), *Cik* (Ms), *Encik* (Mr.) or 'Sir' (another term commonly used by male English teachers in Malaysia), which are more formal. I recall when I was called a 'teacher' and '*cikgu*' in my first few teacher training years in Malaysian secondary schools even when I was only observing lessons conducted by fully fledged teachers (in 2004). In retrospect, from the *relations* (Bucholtz & Hall, 2005) I had with different parties in the schools and filling in a few relief class slots for absent teachers, I had already constructed myself as a teacher who demanded respect from learners as a relatively older 'working' adult in each setting, albeit inexperienced and not doing actual teaching tasks. I drew on and moved my *prospective* (Bernstein, 2000) identity as a teacher into my other existing identities. Despite rather uneventful school observation experience, in a government-sponsored bachelor's degree programme that promised its graduates teaching positions in secondary public schools upon graduation, observing teaching demands in real-life settings then, nonetheless, made me doubt my *prospective* pedagogical identity – whether the teaching profession was for me.

My 'real' teaching experience in a secondary school in Malaysia came only in my final year of the programme in 2007 in an all-girl secondary school in Selangor, Malaysia. I was given the chance to take over the teaching of a Form 4 class of 16-year-old students, mostly came from well-off backgrounds. I then constructed the identity of a young 23-year-old trainee teacher who taught two non-exam classes for about three months. Teaching English language to such learners, many of whom spoke English as their first language, in a premier public school, proved challenging. At first, I remember how frustrating it was as I dwelled on my sense of inferiority as English is my second language, unlike many of my students. I *positioned* (Bucholtz & Hall, 2005) myself as a failed educator when I struggled to even get my students to complete basic homework tasks. From then and still today, I have always felt the need to mask my lack of confidence and non-native proficiency when dealing with high achievers. Upon acknowledging my weakness, after a few weeks, I took pride in being able to rectify the situation by using reverse psychology – I told my students that their work was not as good as the other teachers had told me. The students felt challenged and wanted to prove me wrong. In a farewell party organised by my students for me, they provided me with constructive feedback, that they loved my lessons more than those of their original teacher and would miss me. This experience transformed my *retrospectively* (Bernstein, 2000) sceptical outlook towards the profession, thinking that I was unfit to be a good English teacher, to the *prospective* identity of a promising future as an English teacher. These positive constructions of identities were further reinforced through the 'merit' awarded to me by my supervisor for having excelled in one of my examined teaching sessions. These transformed *positions* and *relations* allowed me to foresee the bright long-term future I might have as a secondary school teacher.

What I thought was going to be a clear career transition to becoming as a secondary school teacher upon graduation was turned upside down by my having to decline my school placement in a rural area, Sabah, in Borneo. I was supposed to teach in a secondary school in a town with no mobile phone connection in 2008, and minimal landline phone access. The whole family was unhappy with the government's arrangements. Two weeks after what I felt was a tragic case of unprecedented breach of contract and unemployment when everyone but me on the TESOL programme immediately became teachers, I applied for a teaching position in a public university in my home state of Kedah. In an instant, my *prospective* identity as a school educator transformed to have an altogether different label, 'lecturer'. Many thought I was *positioned* with an upgraded pedagogical identity, but it was frustrating as I earned a lot less than a secondary school teacher for this part-time position in a university. This circumstance forced me to pursue my master's degree as the only way to earn a reasonable salary and a more stable *prospective* career identity in a tertiary institution.

Labels used for educators in tertiary institutions are not as clear-cut as they may seem to outsiders. In general, just as in most other Western countries, educators in Malaysia are normally referred to as 'lecturers' or '*pensyarah*' but it is uncommon to collocate these terms with educators' first names, unlike the norm in Malaysian schools. Furthermore, the labels also depend on the kind of college or university you teach in. From my observation, it seems that lower-ranked universities or non-research-focused universities award the label 'lecturer' or '*pensyarah*' to educators more easily in their institutions. For example, when I was a new member of the teaching staff with 'just' the qualification of Bachelor of Education (BEd) TESOL in UiTM Kedah, a teaching-focused public university, I was then regarded as a '*pensyarah muda*' (young lecturer). When I later joined UiTM Shah Alam as a permanent member of the academic staff with a master's qualification, I was 'upgraded' to a fully fledged '*pensyarah*' (lecturer) position. Today, as a PhD-qualified educator, I have recently been upgraded to the status of '*pensyarah kanan*' (senior lecturer). In the current context, I no longer draw on my *retrospective* identities as a younger lecturer nor am I drawing on any higher-level *prospective* pedagogical identities as I am now content with how my pedagogical identities turned out. Note that 'young' and 'senior' do not correlate with the educators' age, but their qualifications. Higher-ranked research-focused universities in Malaysia, by contrast, appear to not easily 'award' such professional identities to their academic staff. Educators only get to be called a 'lecturer' or '*pensyarah*' when they have a doctoral degree and involved in an acceptable amount of research work. Otherwise, the educators with degree or master's qualifications are normally termed 'language teachers' (*guru bahasa*) or 'tutors'.

It is also important to address people in Malaysian academia, especially at official functions, using their qualification-related salutations like Dr. or Professor. It is rare for first names to be used by university academic staff in official, semi-formal and even informal settings. There are few exceptions and only based on educators' personal preferences. As a PhD holder of the Centre for Applied Linguistics (CAL), UK, a department that prides itself on its informal relationships between academic staff members (and even with PhD students) in a close-knit group, negotiating my new professional identity in a public university in Malaysia as a lecturer with a doctorate degree, proved challenging. I recalled when I first returned to work in UiTM after passing my viva voce in July 2019 being shocked that some people in my workplace already addressed me as Dr. The situation became more awkward when the official announcements circulated in our official WhatsApp (WA) groups stated officially that my degree had been conferred two months after. Since then, many of my colleagues, even those close to me, address me as Dr. Azrin, even in personal WA messages. There seems to be an unwritten rule that it is safer to use the correct forms of address first upon conferral of an award, and only revert to previous labels (if any) when the addressee him/herself rejects such identities.

As much as I am glad to have completed my PhD, being addressed as Dr. as a part of my professional identity has never really been what motivated me to pursue and complete my studies. This feeling was reinforced further after seeing how the academic staff in CAL managed to maintain professional identities without them being strongly tied to qualification-related forms of address. Even now, after a year since passing my PhD, I am still not comfortable being called Dr. In a less research-focused university like my current workplace where only about 20% of our department's academic staff have PhDs, I feel that such labels have a divisive rather than uniting effect. It seems like I have to learn to *position* (Bucholtz & Hall, 2005) my roles in many ways, by getting used to being called Dr. in most situations and settings in the workplace, whilst maintaining the camaraderie between other, smaller, groups of colleagues, with varying types of qualifications, by removing the academic qualification labels from our names, regardless of our qualifications.

To be relegated to the 'tutor' or 'facilitator' identity *positions* when I was occasionally teaching as a PhD student in the United Kingdom was indeed a unique experience and incredibly humbling. I also feel the labels in a way reflected the pay that I received then. Suffice to state that as a PhD student teaching students – who were pursuing higher qualifications (e.g. undergraduate degree, master's degree and PhD), I was paid much less in the United Kingdom compared to the hourly teaching rates in Malaysia, although understandably, I had more teaching experiences and higher qualifications in the United Kingdom. Indeed, it was an ambivalent experience for me, having to negotiate the identities associated with varied professional labels combined with varying income levels. Even though I later learned that the title 'tutor' in the United Kingdom itself has a wide range of usage and is not necessarily used for less experienced educators, I could not help but feel that such a 'downgrade' would not have happened if I had not decided to teach in the United Kingdom. This is because I was technically still a 'lecturer' even during my PhD studies as I was on unpaid leave then. This helped me realise that professional pedagogical labels are subjective and depend on many factors. Evidently, educators can be awarded random teaching position labels based on many institutional and unavoidable circumstances. In my case, my financial constraints did not leave me much choice and I had to passively accept identities in a different academic and cultural setting. It could thus be that overt professional identities among educators can be constructed in both empowering and delegitimising ways.

Pedagogical Focuses and Styles

Indeed, pedagogical identities extend beyond the labels attached to their positions. In fact, labels only partially address the question of 'what' identities are being constructed, not 'how' they are constructed – arguably the more critical aspect of pedagogical identities.

This is especially relevant when we talk about the pedagogical approaches of L2 educators when they are teaching. In my case, I was trained to be a secondary school English teacher. In terms of lesson planning, I was taught how to write detailed lesson plans, specifying the learning outcomes, sequencing and length of tasks, as well as the teaching materials used. In the Malaysian and UK universities I have taught in, the role of an educator is more of a facilitator. Thus, besides the expected detailed course plans provided, detailed lesson planning for every single class was usually unnecessary.

In terms of university class sizes, the number of students I usually teach is about the same as the number in the public school I once taught in, but I have fewer weekly face-to-face sessions. Malaysian university classrooms generally have more technology facilities than schools, which greatly influence the kinds of lessons conducted. Lessons in universities are expected to be delivered in a variety of ways. Lessons mostly consist of more distant lecture-like learning, while small group tutorials promote more active formal discussions among students. I experienced culture shock relating to these differing teaching requirements and expectations because I still *retrospectively* constructed my identities at the beginning of my career in the university as a school teacher.

In addition, the subject that an educator teaches is another important factor for their construction of identities. The teaching subject may intersect with certain professional labels, for example, the term 'teacher', which is often used for English language teachers in Malaysia and seems a bit odd to generically use 'teacher' if you teach the Malay language (*Bahasa Malaysia*), for example. It is, therefore, no exaggeration to say that the label 'teacher' is almost always exclusively applied to English language educators in Malaysian schools. Even though I later transitioned from schoolteacher to lecturer, I was still basically teaching English proficiency courses involving one or a combination of the four language skills at university. My identities as a language skills educator evolved to become an applied linguistics or content subject educator as a tutor in the University of Warwick. The first experience involved teaching research-related sessions such as how to write literature review and how to analyse qualitative data. Another experience of teaching content subjects for applied linguistics happened in 2018 and 2019 when I agreed to handle tutorial discussions on specific topics within intercultural pragmatics for Hong Kong Open University (HKOU) exchange students. It was nerve-wrecking as my background was not intercultural pragmatics, although I did take pragmatics in my master's study at the Universiti Malaya, Malaysia. To make sure I could teach the sessions well and detach myself temporarily from my *retrospective* identity as a language skills' educator, I had to extensively read many articles to prepare for class discussions, as well as attend the lectures with the students before the tutorials.

Apart from constructing certain institutionalised professional identities and adapting some of my existing pedagogical approaches, I have continued to reinforce some core teaching styles and values held since the beginning of my teaching career. For instance, I still construct myself as an educator with a loud and clearly articulated voice, who always stands whilst teaching. This reflection reveals that educators do have agency to 'pick and choose' – to construct, accept, maintain, reinforce and reject certain pedagogical characteristics, especially those related to teaching approaches. The constructions of other identities, such as those related to demographics, some researchers may argue, are more static. From a social constructionist point of view, the constructions of demographic-related identities are also complex, though in different ways, as discussed later.

Demographic-Related Pedagogical Identities

Educators' Age, Gender, and Marital Status

As shared earlier, I was relatively young when I first addressed and constructed my identity as a lecturer, at 24 years of age. In UiTM Kedah, I perceived myself as a young, single, female lecturer with no tertiary experience. Consequently, I represented myself, and I believed I was perceived by the students, to be a relatively less experienced, but more fun, English language educator. This shows that my varied *positions* could simultaneously render me inferior and superior (in different areas at the same time) in the profession. This phenomenon also reveals the complex negotiations of my pedagogical identities as my age-related and gendered constructions of identities offered me both oppressed and empowering *positions* (Bucholtz & Hall, 2005).

Having trained as a schoolteacher, my university lessons were also unconventional (commented on by my students and colleagues) in the sense that I still held on to some of my *retrospective* identities and beliefs as a school teacher – that English lessons must be fun and active, regardless of settings. For instance, I tried to construct and combine my identities as a young, fun lecturer by letting my students complete grammar practice accompanied by music, which many of the students appeared to appreciate. The feedback from anonymous survey forms that I circulated at the end of the semester showed a small number of my students felt they could not work well in such an environment. Ergo, I learned to be more sensitive to different student learning styles and not impose my own perception of what makes a fun L2 lesson on them.

Gender and its relationship to pedagogical identities can be unpacked by looking at their co-constructions alongside other identities. First, I investigate how the gender of the English language educator can be closely linked to the constructions of professional identities. Unlike many other professions, whether there is 'superior' gender (in terms of numbers, capabilities or both) for teaching English language in Malaysia, the answer is far from straightforward. Personally, I consider female gendered identities in this profession to be normative, but they can also be both legitimising and delegitimising, depending on context. The female English teacher is a normative and thus, an empowering *position* in most countries since female educators almost always make up the majority of English language educators in an institution. In my current workplace itself, about 90% of the English language lecturers are female. This is empowering in that the academy tends to have female leaders in almost all administrative and management positions. The deans over the past 30 years were also mostly females, only very occasionally filled by the few male English language educators the academy had. This is because most university students taking ESL-related courses are female, as this profession is typically associated with nurturance, and thus, femininity (Simpson, 2009). This, however, does not work to female advantage when it comes to competition between applicants for an academic position or promotion in a tertiary institution. From my observation, males seem to have the edge when applying for new jobs or promotion as a language educator when most applicants are female because of their rarity value in this profession. This is the opposite of the female *positions* in a male-majority profession, where females are almost always, in many aspects, delegitimised.

Educators' Ethnic and Religious Identities

The construction and influence of gendered identities in pedagogical positions become even more multifaceted when these identities inescapably intersect with ethnic and religious identities. I construct my ethnic and religious identities as a *Bumiputera* (indigenous people of Malaysia), Malay and Muslim.

I first recall my experience teaching English as a non-veiled female Malay Muslim educator in public and private tertiary institutions in Malaysia. My teaching experience in UiTM Kedah was unique as the university is located in a remote area in Kedah state, in the north of the Malay Peninsula. The majority of the students and staff members were Malay, Muslim and veiled. In fact, I was the only non-veiled Muslim lecturer in the university then and most of my students were veiled as well. It was an awkward *position* to be in, but I was not willing to change my appearance and adopt a veiled physical identity, which although promoted and expected, is not enforced by the university in its constitution. I consciously resisted being mobilised to transform to an expected physical appearance – an identity *position* that I felt did not represent myself. From my colleagues' comments, I had the impression that, despite my daily modest traditional dress to work, usually either a *baju kurung* or a *kebaya*, some of them may have linked my non-veiled identity with their perceptions that (1) I was 'modern'; (2) a city girl raised near the capital city of Kuala Lumpur; (3) educated overseas (i.e. New Zealand); (4) taught English, and hence, was perceived as an L2 educator who incorporated unconventional methods when teaching English to students in the institution.

Later, in 2019, I worked in private institutions in a suburban area of Selangor, the state near the capital, Kuala Lumpur, and the experience was starkly different. All my colleagues then were non-veiled, including another Malay Muslim. Although there was no pressure there to dress in a certain way (in fact all of us mostly wore 'modern Western' clothing of trousers and skirts), my ethnic identity as a Malay in a largely non-Malay institution was challenged. Despite the rapid developments in Malaysia over the past few decades across all races, there is sadly still some form of racial segregation in Malaysia dating from British policy in Malaya before Malaysia's independence (Haniffa,

2017). One of the ongoing stereotyping by a few Malaysians is that ethnic Malays are relatively backwards, and thus are not as good at English as other more economically dominant races in Malaysia like the Chinese and Indians. My students then were mostly Chinese and Indians Malaysians and so, my generic identity as someone from the main and typically privileged ethnic identity in Malaysia shifted to a delegitimised and minority *position*. In one of the first classes, I was challenged by a problematic Chinese student who would not cooperate in learning tasks, and explicitly and implicitly expressed his disappointment at being stuck in an English class taught by a Malay lecturer, rather than Chinese or Indian lecturer like in the two other available classes. Again, I felt defeated and insulted, but I later took that as a challenge to change his perception of me. It was successful and he ultimately became one of the students close to me, so that we kept in touch over social media long after the course ended. Despite the happy ending, the experience taught me the significant impact an educator's ethnic identities may have in the L2 classroom and how it can affect the educator's confidence and performance, as well as be reflected in the lessons, and ultimately linking to the fulfilment of the pre-set learning outcomes.

My religious and ethnic identities as an educator were again challenged in opposing ways when I reflect on my teaching experience in the United Kingdom. In the first one and a half years of my PhD journey starting from October 2015, I consciously rejected the educator identity because I felt the need for rest from pedagogical tasks or identities to focus on completing my PhD as a full-time student. I started getting back to teaching in 2017 when my supervisor strongly encouraged me to handle an NVivo qualitative analysis workshop with the master's students in the department as I was one of her few supervisees who had used NVivo extensively as a research tool. In a way, I was in the face-threatening *position* of not being able to say 'no'. Despite my initial reluctance to re-embrace the identity of an educator at that point, on reflection, I am glad that I did. The experience taught me that educators do have power over which identities they want to construct, though they could also be passively disempowered by being forced to accept certain career identities for circumstantial reasons like financial need or inducement or lack of appropriate human resources.

My understanding of the construction of intersecting intercultural identities also grew by leaps and bounds by my outsider-insider *position* when teaching at the University of Warwick. I was always unsure of my students' perception of me, not only as a *relatively* less qualified educator and a student but also as a visibly female Muslim educator because I had donned the identity of a veiled Muslim female since 2010. I experienced a sense of inferiority which I believe had roots in the typical 'us versus them' discourse notoriously circulated on the media (Coleman & Ross, 2015). I felt as if my physical identity as a minority, a veiled Malaysian Muslim, obviously not of European descent, made me overthink my pedagogical identities in many ways. I imagined my prospective students' disappointment on seeing me on the first day of class, expecting a White European lecturer, but instead having a foreigner to conduct their workshop. I had the idea that the students, especially those who have travelled halfway across the world to study English or linguistics in the United Kingdom would want to be taught by an expert, a local native speaker of English. Upon reviewing more literature in this area, I learned that my insecurities were justified. Many non-Caucasian L2 English educators' ability to teach L2 and related syllabi is judged by their looks and accents (Aneja, 2016).

I constructed myself then not only using the label attached to my specific *position* as an associate or sessional tutor, but also more generally, as an educator and a fellow senior university student in an institution that happened to have, relatively and arguably, more knowledge and skills in the topics presented than I did. I always wondered how my students perceived me. Was I a teacher, a senior student, a lecturer or simply a fellow university mate to them? I dealt with my insecurities about my expert knowledge in the topics I taught (mostly to students I met for the first time) by establishing my teaching credentials and almost ten years of teaching experiences at the beginning of the lesson. That way, I felt more confident and so managed to deliver the sessions more effectively.

After several teaching experiences, I came to view these unique experiences as an advantage – that I get to prove my worth as a veiled Muslim woman able to teach and challenge the expected overt representations of applied linguistics' educators in the Western world – that they are not necessarily White and Christian. On top of such constructions of ethnic and religious identities, I am glad for the exposure of teaching students in a centre that is welcoming in many ways. In addition to the terms of address between colleagues that were inclusive, all PhD students in CAL were regarded as colleagues and given access to the staff pantry (with door pass code to enter at any time!). Such informal relationships between PhD students and academic staff are rare in Malaysian tertiary institutions. Sharing constructs as fellow students in the same institution, though at different levels of academic studies, helped me teach my students there in a more approachable manner. In the end, I was told by the department that the master's students themselves had asked for CAL PhD students to conduct research workshops for them. They felt sharing sessions with the department's own PhD students would give them access to more relevant tips presented in more digestible and practical ways to help them to embark on their dissertation writing journey

When it comes to my intersecting racial and religious identities in my current workplace as an educator, things are less eventful since I work in a monoracial university all *Bumiputeras* who are mostly Muslim. Hence, issues of feeling insecure and awkward surface rarely in this respect. In most cases, I draw on our similarities to come up with clear and interesting lessons, unlike in the United Kingdom, where I took the opportunity to underline my differences in *relation* to them to clarify some terms and grab their attention.

Concluding Remark: What Kind of Educators Are We Now and Will We Be?

If there is one thing educators have learned from teaching during the pandemic in 2020 and 2021, it has to be the realisation that pedagogical identities are contingent and dynamic. As reflected earlier, educators do, to a certain extent, have agency to construct, reinforce, challenge and resist certain identities. However, the kind of educators we are and will be depends on the contextual elements and restrictions around us. The catalyst for changes in pedagogical identities could be the one troubled student in class or something as devastating as a pandemic.

COVID-19 has forced educators to make quick but necessary pedagogical decisions they never imagined possible, consequently constructing pedagogical identities they never associated themselves with. Despite constructing myself as a non-tech savvy educator, I am proud to have recently learned how to conduct online distance learning (ODL) with my students via various video-conferencing platforms, as well as some underexplored but teaching-friendly features in common text messaging applications like WhatsApp (WA) and Telegram. Nevertheless, I keep asking myself: Have I done enough? The endless new webinars shared daily in my workplace emails and WA groups promoting the use of new applications and software seem to suggest 'NO'. Such possibilities are both empowering and overwhelming.

Indeed, educators actively and passively construct, negotiate, resist and challenge multiple intersecting pedagogical identities across diverse academic, cultural and temporal settings. All these settings are central to ensuring aimed learning outcomes and holistic learning are achieved. It is, hence, vital for educators to more critically reflect on their pedagogical identities to facilitate more meaningful L2 teaching and learning. I strongly advocate an increasingly balanced scholarly exploration of educators' identities to provide useful insights into critical aspects of pedagogy.

If I could foresee my pedagogical identities in the next 10 to 25 years, I can confidently predict that I will have constructed myself as a different kind of educator in an unimaginable number of ways. Nonetheless, how I currently conceive of myself and ideally want to be perceived in my academic profession and in this publication, is accessible through my biodata at the beginning of this chapter, which in retrospect, is indeed aptly placed.

References

Abdullah, A. (2002). *Malaysian protocol & correct forms of address*. Times Media Pte Ltd.

Alsup, J. (2008). *Teacher identity discourses: Negotiating personal and professional spaces*. Lawrence Erlbaum Associates, Inc.

Aneja, G. (2016). (Non)native speakered: Rethinking (non)nativeness and teacher identity in TESOL teacher education. *TESOL Quarterly, 50*(3), 572–596. https://doi.org/10.1002/tesq.315

Benwell, B., & Stokoe, E. (2006). *Discourse and identity*. Edinburgh University Press.

Bernstein, B. (2000). *Pedagogy, symbolic control, and identity*. Rowman & Littlefield Publishers.

Bucholtz, M., & Hall, K. (2005). Identity and interaction: A sociocultural linguistic approach. *Discourse Studies, 7*(4–5), 585–614. https://doi.org/10.1177/1461445605054407

Cambridge, J. (2010). The international baccalaureate diploma programme and the construction of pedagogic identity: A preliminary study. *Journal of Research in International Education, 9*(3), 199–213. https://doi.org/10.1177/1475240910383544

Coleman, S., & Ross, K. (2015). *The media and the public*. John Wiley & Sons.

De Fina, A., Schiffrin, D., & Bamberg, M. (2006). *Discourse and identity: Studies in interactional sociolinguistics, 23*. Cambridge University Press.

Dörnyei, Z., & Ushioda, E. (2009). *Motivation, language identity and the L2 self*. Multilingual Matters.

Haniffa, M. (2017). Konflik kaum selepas pendudukan Jepun di tanah melayu: Kajian awal berasaskan sumber lisan. *Journal Peradaban, 10*(1), 16–37. https://doi.org/10.22452/peradaban.vol10no1.2

Lefringhausen, K., Spencer-Oatey, H., & Debray, C. (2019). Culture, norms, and the assessment of communication contexts: Multidisciplinary perspectives. *Journal of Cross-Cultural Psychology, 50*(10), 1098–1111. https://doi.org/10.1177/0022022119889162

Malaysia Map. (2019). *HD world maps*. Retrieved February 9, 2018, from http://world-mapss.blogspot.com/2017/07/malaysia-map.html

Mann, S. (2016). *The research interview: Reflective practice and reflexivity in research processes*. Palgrave Macmillan.

Phan, L. (2008). *Teaching English as an international language*. Multilingual Matters.

Sachs, J. (2001). Teacher professional identity: Competing discourses, competing outcomes. *Journal of Education Policy, 16*(2), 149–161. https://doi.org/10.1080/02680930116819

Simpson, R. (2009). *Men in caring occupations*. Palgrave Macmillan.

Wilson, I., Cowin, L., Johnson, M., & Young, H. (2013). Professional identity in medical students: Pedagogical challenges to medical education. *Teaching and Learning in Medicine, 25*(4), 369–373. https://doi.org/10.1080/10401334.2013.827968

3 The Formation and Development of Teacher Cognition

Zainal, Saiful Izwan

Introduction

Teaching is a talent that, like many others, is primarily acquired through the accumulation of knowledge and experience over a long period of time. It is also important to note that, in the context of tertiary education, the development of an educator's identity and teacher cognition does not begin only with teaching experiences in higher education institutions. Teacher cognition refers to what instructors know, think, believe and do in their classrooms. In light of the fact that teacher cognition cannot be observed, previous studies have concentrated on observing teachers' teaching practices, conducting interviews with teachers to better understand their thinking styles, and a variety of other methods to gain a thorough understanding of the dimensions of teacher cognition (Borg, 2006).

Teacher cognition is an essential element of education that deserves greater attention and consideration if we are to address major problems and challenges connected to teaching at any level in a comprehensive manner. Because it includes elements of an educator's beliefs, knowledge and style of thinking, teacher cognition is essential because these characteristics will directly or indirectly influence the teacher's identity, as well as techniques and approaches in the classroom (Borg, 2006). Moreover, according to Borg (2006), a variety of variables, including contextual circumstances, schooling, teacher education and the surrounding culture, must be taken into consideration in the development of a teacher's cognition and teaching practice.

My cognitive development as an educator will be fully explored in this chapter, which will begin with my early education and continue until my latest teacher training. As an educator, I will discuss the connection between the exposure I had during that time period and the development of my cognition as a teacher. Following that, I will reflect on my professional educational path, which began as a teacher in a government school, up until my current profession as a senior lecturer at a public university in Malaysia.

DOI: 10.4324/9781003374190-3

The Relationship Between the Experience as a Student and the Formation of Teacher Cognition: Early Interest in Teaching

A person's experiences and information gained as a student will either directly or indirectly influence the development of his or her teacher cognition, according to the teacher cognition framework presented by Borg (2003) (see Figure 3.1). He added that improvements in teacher cognition are difficult to achieve, but they are nevertheless achievable. Even if one's previous experiences and information as a student have a major part in forming one's teacher cognition, Ertmer (2005) asserts that a person's beliefs and beliefs systems will still be filtered by fresh knowledge and experience. The belief of an individual

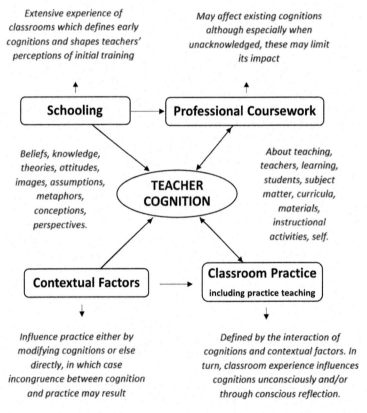

Extensive experience of classrooms which defines early cognitions and shapes teachers' perceptions of initial training

May affect existing cognitions although especially when unacknowledged, these may limit its impact

Schooling ─────► **Professional Coursework**

Beliefs, knowledge, theories, attitudes, images, assumptions, metaphors, conceptions, perspectives.

TEACHER COGNITION

About teaching, teachers, learning, students, subject matter, curricula, materials, instructional activities, self.

Contextual Factors ────► **Classroom Practice** including practice teaching

Influence practice either by modifying cognitions or else directly, in which case incongruence between cognition and practice may result

Defined by the interaction of cognitions and contextual factors. In turn, classroom experience influences cognitions unconsciously and/or through conscious reflection.

Figure 3.1 Teacher cognition, schooling, contextual factors, professional education and classroom practice (Borg, 1997 as cited in Borg, 2003, p. 82)

is a personal notion, according to him, yet it is firmly entrenched, immovable and difficult to alter. The authors, Windschitl and Sahl (2002), agree with this assertion, stating that previous teaching experiences give instructors with a conceptual model for teaching that has a substantial impact on a person's teaching behaviours and practices in the future.

Several past studies have shown that teachers' experiences, when they were students in the early stages of schooling, have a significant impact on their current and future teaching practices and teacher cognition. For example, Windschitl and Sahl (2002) found that most teachers face problems adopting constructivist methods because most of them went through traditional learning processes when they were growing up. This creates a gap between teachers and students, resulting in teachers becoming more comfortable using conventional teaching methods due to their past learning experiences. This situation poses a great challenge for such educators since students of this age, in contrast, prefer learning techniques that incorporate the use of digital technology (Che Had & Ab Rashid, 2019). Teachers who are exposed to the use of digital technology in the early stages of their learning will usually be agents of change who tend to use the technology in teaching and try to meet the current needs of students, rather than using traditional methods (Che Had & Ab Rashid, 2019). In my own experience, I have been drawn to the usage of digital technology since I was a child, owing to the early exposure I had in this area from my parents. During my childhood, my father worked as the coordinator of the teacher activity centre, where he was responsible for the use of digital technology tools such as computers, video cameras and other such devices. My exposure to digital technology tools began indirectly when I was a child, and when I became an educator, the usage of digital technology tools became a natural option for me, and I felt completely at ease with them. This indicates that experience during schooling years has a significant impact on the formation of teacher cognition.

The element of my experience as a student is, in fact, very closely linked to the development of my teacher cognition, particularly from the perspective of my predisposition towards the area of education. My parents were both high school teachers while I was growing up. Because I grew up in a household with a large number of educators, I was exposed to a variety of unique situations that have helped to mould me into the type of educator I am today. However, as far back as I can remember, growing up as the child of educators did not immediately pique my interest in pursuing a career in the teaching field. Growing up and being 'observed' and 'valued' by society as the 'teachers' child' produced mixed feelings for me, to put it mildly. There were moments when it was enjoyable and others when it was not.

When you are the child of parents who are both teachers, one of the benefits of being their child is having access to an extensive supply of instructional materials. My parents often received a large number of free books and teaching materials from a variety of sources for the purpose of teaching. In this way, I was exposed to a wide range of academic literature from an early age, as well as having access to additional learning resources that were otherwise unavailable to the majority of my schoolmates at the time of my education. The fact that my 'observations' on how to teach began as a result of this exposure is unavoidable in my opinion. Due to my parents' experiences as teachers in public secondary schools, I had a better understanding of the work culture and ethics of educators, including the significance of having an excellent personality and being completely trustworthy in the performance of duties. In addition, I started to appreciate their enthusiasm and dedication to their profession as a teacher. I could sense and see that they were passionate about teaching, and that this intrinsic drive enabled them to be content in their everyday teaching duties, despite the difficulties they encountered. Apart from that, I was constantly reminded to behave properly and obtain great academic achievements in order to preserve the good name and reputation of my parents as teachers from an early age, which I did. Although this situation was a hardship to me, I did not consider it to be such since, more than likely, I would have chosen the same career path even if my parents had not been educators.

To be clear, my drive and desire to earn my livelihood by teaching began at an early age for which I am grateful. When it came to remembering and revising what I had learned in the classroom, one of the methods I used was to teach others. As a result, I was always on the lookout for chances to share my knowledge with my siblings, relatives, and friends whenever the opportunity presented itself. Over time, a passion that began as a casual pastime evolved into something more defined and significant. In particular, when others seemed to grasp what I was trying to teach them, I felt a feeling of fulfilment that fuelled my desire to continue teaching them.

When I entered high school, I had already served in a number of roles, including class monitor and prefect, among others. The activities associated with such roles sometimes included peer mentoring activities, in which I was tasked with instructing peers on topics relevant to the courses we were studying at the time. Such activities helped me to realise that the teaching process is not without its difficulties. It is necessary to use the appropriate methods and approaches in order for the individual being taught to really comprehend what is being taught. In the beginning, I utilised a lot of popular songs to teach English to my friends and cousins, which was quite effective. One of the methods I employed at the time was lyric memorisation, which helped me to speed up the process of learning sentence patterns and vocabulary items. I remember that at the time, we listened to popular songs on our 'Walkmans' and old cassette radio players, and we were able to memorise and sing the songs as a result of this method. Despite the fact that cassettes were incredibly expensive for high school students at the time, we were ready to spend money on things that we were passionate about. Starting from that point on, my relatives and friends, who had previously shown apprehension about learning English, began to express an interest, particularly when they realised that their comprehension of and performance in English were increasing. Initially, I attempted to teach by trial and error since I was unfamiliar with any teaching philosophy. However, when I saw that some of my efforts were yielding results, I took note and felt extremely pleased. These good changes also had a major effect on my confidence in my ability to teach, and I have subsequently shown an interest in pursuing a career as a teacher.

Aside from that, it is important to note that I started to exhibit an interest in writing during the first year of my high school education, particularly in the Malay language. When I placed first in a writing competition at the state level, my passion in the subject became even greater. From that point on, I started to demonstrate a strong desire to expand my understanding of and improve my proficiency in the language. Because of my active involvement in co-curricular activities such as contests at the national level, my tendency continued to improve. I also became interested in counselling and leadership as a result of my involvement in motivational events organised by the school and the Ministry of Education. I am glad that all of my inclinations and experiences at the time increased my confidence and helped me realise my goal of becoming an educator.

In Form 4 (10th grade, 16 years old), I was given the opportunity to continue my studies in a boarding school in the same area, and that was where I spent my last years of schooling. At that school, I started to get used to the arena of debate. Through debates, I acquired a variety of techniques for increasing my self-confidence while speaking in public. Prior to then, I was a very timid person who avoided participation in events that needed me to speak in front of a group of people. My important experience in debate has definitely helped to alleviate my initial sense of intimidation while speaking in front of a large group of people, and it has also helped to increase my confidence in my pursuit of a teaching career.

Borg (2006) emphasised the importance of substantial classroom experience in the development of teacher cognition. As far as I can recall, the majority of the teachers that taught me were very compassionate and dedicated to their students. Perhaps it was simply a coincidence, but the teachers who taught me during my school years often provided me with pleasant experiences, which led me to admire some of them and aspired to be like them. Even if there were instances in which teachers engaged in unprofessional behaviour, such occurrences were very rare.

In conclusion, the experiences, knowledge and exposure I received since childhood have directly or indirectly influenced the formation of my teacher cognition. Furthermore, the exposure to the learning culture I received also shaped my thinking styles and choices in determining which teaching methods to be used in diverse teaching contexts. This is in line with the claim made by Borg (2006), who relates the experience during the schooling years with the preferences and style of thinking of a teacher, especially in the aspect of teaching.

Teacher Training at the University and Teacher Training Institute

Past studies have shown a significant relationship between teacher education and teacher cognition (Borg, 2003; Ertmer & Ottenbreit-Leftwich, 2010). Borg (2011) states that teacher cognition influences not only a teacher's teaching practices but also their beliefs and cognition.

Indeed, the experiences and information I acquired throughout my teacher training have had a significant impact on the development of my teacher cognition. As soon as I graduated from high school, I was offered a scholarship to continue my education as part of a twinning programme between a teacher training institute in Malaysia and Macquarie University in Sydney, Australia, majoring in a Bachelor of Education (TESOL). It was then that I started my formal education in the area of education, in preparation for realising my lifelong goal of becoming an educator.

Ertmer and Ottenbreit-Leftwich (2010) stated that teacher education has a great impact in shaping a teacher's teaching practices. I agree with this statement as my undergraduate degree programme had indeed provided me with the opportunity to delve into more detailed teaching methods. At the beginning of my learning phase at the teacher training institute, I was exposed to various theories and methods related to the teaching processes. According to Borg (2003) (refer to Figure 3.1), professional coursework can have an impact on a person's existing cognition. As a result of my learning about teaching theories and methods, I was able to make connections between different teaching methods and the reasons why they should be used in particular situations. Through a knowledge of those causes, I was able to better comprehend students' psychological and developmental elements, which play a critical role in the teaching and learning process. I also had the opportunity to relate what I learned to my previous experiences as a school student. In those processes of reflection, I somehow did not try to find the best methods to teach effectively but I was more focused on understanding the best methods to identify student needs. I was often reminded of the methods my teachers used in school and tried to emulate what they had used in terms of helping students based on their needs. As I previously mentioned, I was lucky to have met a number of very devoted teachers during my schooling years, all of whom serve as role models for me in the field of education. Through observations, I could see quite noticeable differences between students in schools in different areas. Factors such as ethnicity, type of community, family background, socioeconomic background, social networking and so on were seen to play a very important role in determining the appropriate teaching methods to use (Borg, 2003). Before being exposed to such experiences, I already had a mindset regarding teaching methods that I felt were ideal for students, but after understanding the realities that occur in schools from different regions, I began to realise that many factors need to be considered before designing and when applying certain methods in teaching.

In Sydney, where I was studying for my undergraduate degree, I had the chance to see a society that was very different from the one I was used to in Malaysia. While I was there, I learned more about how important it is to recognise the requirements of individual children as well as the techniques that can be used to meet those needs so that no one is left behind. Additionally, I got the chance to learn about different teaching techniques that made use of digital technology tools. This significant exposure completely changed my perspective on the possibility of utilising technology to achieve desired outcomes in the classroom. In terms of the use of digital technology in the classroom, I discovered that it is critical for teachers to be aware of their students' socioeconomic and sociocultural backgrounds before choosing and implementing suitable digital technology tools in their courses.

When I returned to Malaysia from Sydney, I was given the chance to do my teaching practicum in a secondary school in Kajang, a district in the state of Selangor. At first, I was apprehensive about beginning my teaching career at the school. Several pupils at the school were often engaged in criminal cases involving the police, and the few of them were from families who ran gangsterism activities in and around Kuala Lumpur, I was told by a school official. When I first arrived at the school, several instructors warned me that I would need to be extra cautious and patient with certain students since they were prone to acting out of control and aggressive in school.

My teaching experience at the school started on a rather threatening note. On the first day of my teaching, some students, in fact, tried to make fun of me and disrupted the concentration of other students when I was teaching. Upon learning that the majority of their classmates did not approve of their actions, they decided to cease their behaviour altogether. Although it seemed to be a fortunate situation for classroom management, it resulted in additional difficulties in the learning process. Due to the low level of engagement among my students in the classroom, my following teaching sessions were more teacher-centred, which was problematic. Despite the fact that my pupils did not exhibit any disciplinary issues in my class, they were mostly passive when requested to engage in the activities that were given to them. They also did not demonstrate a fair level of understanding for the subject matter that I had taught them, which was much less than what I had anticipated. Some students were uninterested in participating in every activity I planned and chose to remain seated while the instructional sessions were taking place. Some of them decided not to respond when I administered a test, while others fell asleep throughout the course of the test session. I voiced my problems to some of the teachers there, and they advised me to be firm with the students and implement the school corporal punishment. I, however, felt uncomfortable with such an approach as it went against my beliefs in teaching and the positive teaching vibes that I have observed from my parents since I was a child. I, therefore, decided not to accept and apply a different approach in my class. I decided to try implementing more pragmatic and humanistic approaches with my students in the class. For example, in order to be closer to and understand my students, I decided to organise a small party for them. With my relatively limited budget, I bought chicken rice, drinks and several types of snacks for all the students and asked the students to arrange their classes for the small party. Most of the students showed great interest in organising the party and eagerly helped me at that time. From this situation, I could see that some students who had previously been less willing to cooperate had begun to show a tendency to participate. During the party, I organised some language activities and a sharing session. From there, I could see changes in my students who were previously quite rebellious during my learning sessions. They were increasingly showing interest in participating and started asking questions if they did not understand the topics that I taught then. They were also increasingly more competitive and critical in trying to address the questions that I posed at that time. As the party progressed, I took the opportunity to chat with some students who previously had been less cooperative with me during my lessons. At first, our interaction was a bit awkward; however, they became increasingly friendly with me after a while, and some of them started sharing their true feelings and life situations with me. Starting from that moment, I began to understand the dilemma that some of my students had to endure, which I had never thought of before. From my interactions with them, I found that many of them came from troubled families. They were facing many serious social problems at home and in their surroundings, ranging from issues such as parental divorce, poverty, involvement with gangsterism, and a lack of parental attention. Only then I realised how much my students have taught me about being an educator and about life in general. I gained the most crucial knowledge as an educator, which is not to judge students only based on their attitudes in the classroom. This is because, in reality, most educators do not know what is going on in their students' lives outside school. Similar to what Borg (2003) stated in his framework (see Figure 3.1), contextual factors will have an impact on a teacher's cognition and practises. In the situation I encountered, the experience reinforced my belief in the importance of understanding students' backgrounds, while also assisting me in doing so more accurately.

Fortunately, party was successful and the students I taught started to become more friendly and close with me. Also, surprisingly, they started to focus a lot better during my lessons in the classroom. From that experience, I found that the interaction and efforts of teachers to get to know their students is very important to build a sense of care, love and rapport with them. The experience has also taught me the significance of establishing mutual respect and understanding between students and teachers in the teaching and learning process. I began to realise that a teacher's knowledge of a student's circumstances and needs would be constructive in determining the appropriate approach to take when developing a student's learning potential. After that experience, unfortunately, I only had the opportunity to teach my students for a few weeks due to the short teaching practicum period. I, however, had gained some instrumental and invaluable knowledge that I can apply throughout my career as an educator.

My interest in becoming an educator grew as a result of nearly six years of undergraduate study in the field of education in both Malaysian and Australian educational settings, during which I became increasingly passionate about becoming an educator. I was, and continue to be, acutely aware of the fact that being an educator in this day and age is becoming increasingly difficult. In spite of this, I believe that the knowledge and experiences I gained during that time have given me greater courage, tenacity and the wisdom that I require in order to become a more effective educator.

The Influence of Contextual Factors on Teacher Cognition

According to Borg (2006), contextual factors influence the formation of teacher cognition, and the situation is dynamic; continues to change from time to time. Numerous previous studies described the importance of teaching context in the formation of teacher cognition, and some evidence has confirmed that contextual factors provide a hindering and facilitative impact on teaching (Cuayahuitl & Carranza, 2015; Jamalzadeh & Shahsavar, 2015). This statement aligns with Borg's (2006) claim, which states that there is a clear correlation between teachers' practices, beliefs and knowledge with contextual factors. Borg (2006) also adds that the instructional, social and institutional setting in which a teacher works also has a very significant impact on their cognition and practices.

More recent research has shown a persistent connection between sociopsychological variables and teacher cognition in a variety of settings. For example, in a study conducted by Sanches and Borg (2014), socio-cultural, environmental and psychological factors directly or indirectly influence second language (L2) teachers' pedagogical decisions. In a different study, Johnson et al. (2012) showed that the context related to the work environment has a more significant impact on teacher cognition than financial considerations.

Relating these findings to my own experiences, contextual factors have indeed greatly influenced my teacher cognition. My teaching career journey began in 2008 when I was officially appointed to work as an English teacher at a public secondary school in the district of Muar, Johor in the south of Malaysia. My feelings at that time were very mixed; there was the excitement of taking my first steps in the teaching profession, and also there was this overwhelming sense of nervousness because I did not know what I was going to face.

The secondary school in which I first taught was located in the suburban area. I was assigned to teach classes which had students with relatively poor English language proficiency and performance. Many of my students stated that they were not interested and were afraid of learning English. The education minister at that time, Datuk Seri Mahdzir Khalid, also stated that this matter is common in most schools in Malaysia, where many students have problems in English, especially in the aspect of speaking (Zazali, 2017). I saw that situation as an opportunity for me to apply what I have learned informally when I was much younger and also formally when I was in the university. I planned some strategies to bring the students closer to the English subject. In the early stages, I used entertaining activities such as using videos, music and playing musical instruments to get my students' attention. The techniques managed to gain the attention and interest of most of my students then, and they started memorising English songs and speaking more in English. Most of them also began to show interest in studying more diligently and concentrating in during English lessons. For students who had a moderate level of proficiency in English, I encouraged them to participate in several competitions at the district level, and the results were very much gratifying. Many of them achieved excellent results at the district level, defeating the participants from the many other 'elite' schools in the district. From such experiences, I learned that if we can eliminate the fear of trying to use English among our students and cultivate their interest through their own achievements, the learning process will take place on their own volition. When students can see their own academic improvements, they will continue to feel motivated and improve their performance on their own, even without anyone's encouragement.

In addition to focusing on the English subject alone, I also tried to forge closer ties and build rapport with the students I taught, by inviting them to join the softball team that I set up. In addition to fulfilling my job scope for co-curricular activities, I used the opportunity to reach out to weaker students, so that we could get to know each other better. This approach seemed to work because the weaker students began to get closer to me and showed more interest while learning English in class. As a bonus from that approach, the newly formed softball team earned an outstanding place in competitions at the district level, and several students were called up to represent the district to compete at the state level. In the same year, I received an award for successfully improving students' performance in English in the national examination for three consecutive years. I was and am grateful and feel honoured for such a recognition. Ultimately, however, what really has been an invaluable and satisfying teaching accomplishment for me is witnessing my students' change from being rebellious and not interested in learning English to showing genuine interest in learning English. When reflecting on the approach that I have practised when teaching and mentoring my students then, clearly, they were all based on the knowledge and experience that I had gained during my schooling years and teacher training, in addition to being influenced by some contextual factors.

After serving at the public school for almost five years, I took a very difficult decision in 2012. Due to an unavoidable family issue (my dream to live together with my wife and my son in the same household after living apart for two years), I decided to tender my resignation as a public-school teacher with the Ministry of Education Malaysia. Using my master's qualification (in Educational Management) that I attained from my part-time studies while I was working as a teacher, I managed to secure a job position as a lecturer. I worked at a private university in the urban area in the state of Selangor where my wife and son lived. Then began a new episode for me as an educator at a tertiary institution, at which I had to plan, develop and apply new approaches to teach adult learners effectively.

Teaching at a private university in urban areas has also provided me with some unique experiences in many other different ways. In the beginning, I used the same approaches that I had used before in schools. However, I have later learnt first-hand from this experience that educators need to understand the socioeconomic and socio-cultural backgrounds of the students (Borg, 2003). Most of my students in the university came from well-to-do and moderate backgrounds. In terms of their proficiency in English, most of them actually had a fairly good command. Accordingly, my role has transitioned to more of a facilitator who focuses more on managing activities in the classroom. My focus was no longer on enriching language skills, but rather on providing appropriate training for students so that they can use English for specific purposes. Working at a private university also required me to do some assignments involving marketing, advertising, etc. These extra assignments initially put an additional burden on me, as they were not related to teaching. Still, the longer I became accustomed to such tasks, the more I understood the field of education from a financial point of view and the importance of maintaining the best quality of education.

A few years later, I received another scholarship to further my studies at the doctoral level in the United Kingdom, and shortly after graduation, I was offered a position as a senior lecturer at a public university, and I have been working there until now. Throughout and after the PhD learning process, I had the chance to learn about and analyse a variety of scenarios involving the learning and teaching process, which both directly and indirectly reinforced my prior views and knowledge. Even though I have had the chance to study in detail from professionals in the field of education, I still believe that there is much more information that I need to acquire in order to be really competent in understanding the actual needs of students in a classroom setting. What I can conclude is that the needs of students vary over time because many variables such as students' evolving talents, changes in their backgrounds, changes in their socioeconomic circumstances, changes in their thought processes, and so on, influence the needs of the students through time. As a result, I believe that a teacher's efforts to continue to provide the greatest possible education to their students must be ongoing, and that continual learning and training must take place in order to guarantee that their skills are constantly current and relevant from time to time.

Conclusion

Several scholars such as Borg (2003) and Li (2020) have reiterated the indispensable, dynamic and interlinked roles of an educator's familial and educational backgrounds, teaching beliefs, teaching environment, teaching practices, identities and teacher cognition in achieving a holistic teaching and learning experience. My reflections have exemplified and reinforced the significant impact of each of these factors on the teacher cognition. Finding that the information and expertise I have gained during my learning and teaching process is always in a flexible state, I find that I am always required to make adjustments in response to changing conditions and requirements. That is to say that the teaching techniques I am required to employ are not static, but must be continuously dynamic as time progresses in order to keep up with changes in teaching technology, changing requirements of students, and a variety of other variables. Additionally, the abilities I need must be continually developed in order for me to stay relevant and at a level that enables me to assist students in their academic endeavours.

References

Borg, S. (2003). Teacher cognition in language teaching: A review of research on what language teachers think, know, believe, and do. *Language Teaching, 36*, 81–109.

Borg, S. (2006). *Teacher cognition and language education: Research and practice.* Continuum.

Borg, S. (2011). The impact of in-service teacher education on language teachers' beliefs. *System, 39*(3), 370–380.

Che Had, M., & Ab Rashid, R. (2019). A review of digital skills of Malaysian English language teachers. *International Journal of Emerging Technologies in Learning (IJET), 14*(2), 139.

Cuayahuitl, R. E., & Carranza, P. C. (2015). Influence of contextual factors on EFL Mexican teachers' beliefs and the use of textbooks. *HOW, 22*(2), 75–90.

Ertmer, P. (2005). Teacher pedagogical beliefs: The final frontier in our quest for technology integration? *Educational Technology Research and Development, 53*(4), 25–39.

Ertmer, P., & Ottenbreit-Leftwich, A. T. (2010). Teacher technology change: How knowledge, confidence, beliefs, and culture intersect. *Journal of Research on Technology in Education, 42*(3), 255–284.

Jamalzadeh, M., & Shahsavar, Z. (2015). The effects of contextual factors on teacher's beliefs and practices. *Procedia-Social and Behavioral Sciences, 192*(4), 166–171.

Johnson, S. M., Kraft, M. A., & Papay, J. P. (2012). How context matters in high-need schools: The effects of teachers' working conditions on their professional satisfaction and their students' achievement. *Teaching College Record, 114*(10), 1–39.

Li, L. (2020). *Language teacher cognition: A sociocultural perspective* [Ebook]. Springer Nature Limited. Retrieved May 31, 2021, from https://doi.org/10.1057/978-1-137-51134-8.

Sanches, H. S., & Borg, S. (2014). Insights into L2 teachers' pedagogical content knowledge: A cognitive perspective on their grammar explanations. *System, 44*(1), 45–53. https://doi.org/10.1016/j.system.2014.02.005

Windschitl, M., & Sahl, K. (2002). Tracing teachers' use of technology in a laptop computer school: The interplay of teacher beliefs, social dynamics, and institutional culture. *American Educational Research Journal, 39*(1), 165–205.

Zazali Musa. (2017). Students must overcome fear of speaking English, says Mahdzir. *The Star*. Retrieved May 31, 2021, from www.thestar.com.my/news/nation/2017/10/02/students-must-overcome-fear-of-speaking-english-says-mahdzir.

4 Experiencing Teaching in the United Kingdom

Ab Rahman, Nur Afiqah

Introduction

This chapter describes my teaching experiences in Malaysia and the United Kingdom. I try to capture the opportunities and challenges that I faced in teaching in a country that has a different learning landscape by giving an insider-outsider perspective. At times, I observed as an insider that lived in the United Kingdom. Other times, I took perspective as a Malaysian and observed as an outsider. I draw upon what I have learned about the similarities and differences in regard to pedagogy, culture and professional development in the education system in both countries.

Education in Malaysia

I will briefly explain the education system in Malaysia to set the context for my personal experience in this chapter.

Malaysia is a multiracial society that consists of Bumiputra (largely Malay), Chinese, Indian and other ethnic groups. In 2022, Malay covers 69.9% of the population while Chinese, Indian and other ethnic groups cover 22.8%, 6.7% and 0.7%, respectively (Current Population Estimates, 2022). The diverse cultural and ethnic landscape in Malaysia is reflected in its education system as schools in Malaysia admit students regardless of their backgrounds. This diversity brings students' unique identities yet sharing similar values as Malaysians. I taught in a school in which Malay pupils dominated the school, followed by Chinese, Indian and the natives of Sabah and Sarawak.

I also worked as a part-time lecturer in HE in Malaysia, hence I will provide the context for HE in Malaysia as well. Malaysian HE is largely attended by Malaysians but with an increase diversity of international students. As of 2021, 94.23% local students and 5.77% international students enrolled in public universities (Quick Facts, 2021). There is no data found on the origins of the international students. I work as a tutor in the United Kingdom, so it is fair that I provide the context for the UK HE as well. As a comparison, in 2021, the HE in the United Kingdom consists of 78% of local UK students, 5.56%

DOI: 10.4324/9781003374190-4

of European Union (EU) students and 16.4% of non-European Union students (HE Student Enrolments by Domicile, 2022). Both EU and non-EU are considered as international students.

My Teaching Experience

My teaching experience is multifaceted. I have experienced teaching in schools and HE in both Malaysia and the United Kingdom.

In Malaysia, I worked as a teacher in a primary school. I also worked as a part-time lecturer in private and public universities, teaching academic skills and English courses to undergraduates. I taught local and international students, coming from diverse backgrounds with an age range from 17 to 60 years. In the school I worked at, the pupils were all Malaysians and in the universities I taught, in every lecture, there were fewer than five international students out of approximately 30–40 students. In the United Kingdom, I worked as a tutor, delivering academic skills workshops, face-to-face and online, to foundation, undergraduate and postgraduate students.

The New Working Culture

My teaching experience in the United Kingdom began once I attended the induction meeting for my job. It was there where I had the opportunities to meet other tutors and put faces to the names that I had come across on our email corresponds. I imagined I would get to know them, to know what their backgrounds were, and their teaching experiences. I was wrong. The context of interaction was something I had never experienced before. Usually, in my home country, I would ask questions like 'Where are you from? Which department are you working at? Where did you work previously?' to start a conversation. However, during this meeting, I froze. I was worried whether these questions were inappropriate to ask. I was aware of the personal-professional boundary that was part of the British culture, something that was unusual to Malaysian culture. It was challenging as I had the dilemma between trying to network but concerned about cultural differences.

The uneasiness I felt is not unusual. Culture has been defined as "a fuzzy set of assumptions and values, orientations to life, beliefs, policies, procedures and behavioural conventions that are shared by a group of people, and that influence (but do not determine) each member's behaviour and his/her interpretations of the 'meaning' of other people's behaviour" (Spencer-Oatey, 2008, p. 3). Understanding culture is not a straightforward affair. Instead, it requires frequent exposure with the particular society to learn more about their culture. Thus, to overcome the uneasiness that I felt, I made an effort to engage in conversation, focusing on understanding cultural similarities and differences. I consciously observed what people talked about when conversing and how they behaved in different situations. I learned to not ask questions that might cause discomfort – for example, about ethnicity, position or family.

One important thing that I noticed was most of the time, being polite was key. If I was unsure about the appropriateness of a question, I always began by apologising, explaining the purpose of the question and giving the other person the option of not answering my question if they did not want to. My behaviour is expected as explained by Spencer-Oatey and Kadar (2021) about intercultural interaction. They made a point of how having an intercultural interaction may bring politeness into the act of communication as "people seek to maintain smooth relationships . . . or establish new relationships" (p. 4).

Referring back to the induction meeting, it lasted for an hour. Other than the opportunity to meet other tutors, the meeting was set as an opportunity for tutors to learn about accessing Moodle as the main hub for teaching materials. The tutors were also briefed on the courses that needed to be completed online as part of the induction. Additionally, tutors were given links to relevant and important information about university policies and culture that needed to be known. We were informed that trainings would be in the form of observing other tutors' lessons.

There are three things I would like to point out here – the manner of conducting an induction, the trainings given and the practice of creating culture.

In public services in Malaysia, induction is seen as an important part of starting a new job. It is a common practice that new staff are expected to attend a week (or so) of training filled with various face-to-face courses and activities to help them understand the nature of their work. The courses vary from one institution to another, and the selection of the courses depends on the position of the new staff attending the induction as these courses focus on facilitating the new staff on performing their role. Organising an induction is time consuming, costly, and involves people of different expertise. As such, it is not conducted on a regular basis. Some new staff need to wait a few months before they can attend an induction. Acknowledging these restrictions, the Ministry of Education Malaysia has changed their approach. They start giving out CDs containing relevant courses for induction for new teachers to access, and the teachers are required to complete assignments to pass the induction. However, many other institutions still practise the face-to-face induction. I would like to mention here that this nature of induction might change in the future as the effect of the Covid19 pandemic.

Induction in the United Kingdom is a different story. As explained earlier, the face-to-face meeting was an opportunity to brief and introduce tutors. I was given an induction kit that was meant to be explored individually. Included in the pack was a checklist of online courses that I needed to complete and information that I needed to read in my own time. The same checklist was provided for new staff regardless of their position. I could see that the focus of the induction was to create a workplace culture in which all staff must be aware of important rules and information of the institution. The courses included standard guidelines on how to react to issues that might arise when in contact with students and other staff. This includes safeguarding, equality and diversity, fire safety and data protection regulations. Some courses had assessment where there was a minimum score to pass. Once I have completed the courses and read all information, I only need to tick the boxes and email the checklist to my line manager. The manner in which induction is conducted shows that trust and honesty are paramount. Line managers trust new staff in completing the checklist and new staff being honest about completing the induction as required without being monitored physically. Trust and honesty are traits that are instilled unconsciously as parts of creating culture.

Once the induction has been completed, I was then required to attend trainings before I could teach any courses. The trainings were actually a series of observation on the teaching of other tutors. Attending trainings allowed me to examine the lessons from multiple perspectives and justify the tutors' actions. The content was pre-designed. However, I could see that the tutors 'owned' the course even though it was their first time teaching for the course. It showed that they really knew the content of the courses by heart. They were familiar with the flow of content, the assessments and explanations for the slides. They worked hard to understand the content that they did not create themselves. Bear in mind, the level of understanding and familiarity is different when we prepare our own lecture notes compared to when someone prepares it for us. When we prepare well, confidence follows. Although we might be confident in one area and weaker in another (Quigley, 2016).

Other than teaching responsibilities, educators are expected to exemplify good behaviour to students. Punctuality is a key component of these responsibilities. Educators are expected to start lessons on time. However, this is not always the case. In every training that I observed, the tutors waited a few minutes for other students to arrive before they started the course. This attitude showed that they tolerated tardiness and empathy by considering that students might have other lectures previously or have to walk from different parts of the campus. They appreciated the students' effort to coming to the course given that the course did not contribute to their grade. Nonetheless, when students were late and missed the essential parts of the course as a consequence, students were advised to join the next available session, to make sure they could learn meaningfully.

Being a teacher for so many years, I always believed that I must be on time, start my lesson as planned and keep to my plan. Being able to observe other tutors' doing, I learned that being empathetic and creating a positive relationship ease the process of learning. Creating positive relationships is the first part of the 'house metaphor' described by Whitaker et al. (2018). They picture classroom management as the house we live in which consists of 'the foundation' (relationship), 'the structure' (high and clear expectation) and 'the maintenance' (regular upkeep). The foundation for a house must be strong to allow the house to be built. Similarly, in a classroom, a positive relationship will ease the process of transmitting information to the students. Positive relationships will also help in preventing bad behaviour (Emmer & Sabornie, 2015; Hamre et al., 2008).

Referring back to the observation, the tutors started the course by asking students to write the reasons why they attended the course. By doing so, the tutors were considering the students' needs before they started the teaching. As the course was open to all students, it was crucial for the tutors to make sure they cater to what the students needed for their skills and self-development. Most of the time, tutors were able to relate the course objectives with the students' needs. At times, when there were less students, tutors were able to make adjustments to the course to cater to the small group of attendees. Whichever the cases were, tutors would explain the learning outcomes. Setting a clear expectation echoed 'the structure' used in the house metaphor (Whitaker et al., 2018) explained earlier. Informing the learning outcomes will prepare the students on what they should achieve by the end of the lesson. Having clear learning outcomes allow tutors to plan activities and assessments for the lesson. This pattern is described as the concept of constructive alignment, an outcome-based learning developed by Biggs and Tang (2007). This concept focuses on aligning learning outcomes, learning activities and assessment to facilitate learners in constructing their learning.

Throughout the observation, I could see that the tutors maintained the students' focus by asking questions, probing responses and facilitating various individual and group activities. The approach of consistently checking students' understanding is related to 'the maintenance' in the house metaphor (see Whitaker et al., 2018). In this case, the concept of maintenance can be seen from the tutors' efforts in assessing understanding and identifying problems throughout the lesson, rather than waiting till the end. The communication occurred during the teaching and learning process was also parallel to the concept of 'the maintenance' which is to consistently build this relationship.

Observing other tutors was a valuable experience that I had. Throughout my teaching career in Malaysia, being observed at least yearly by superiors for assessment purposes was a routine. However, observing colleagues as a learning process was uncommon. I did not realise that observing colleagues was indeed beneficial for my professional development. There is always something new that I can learn from others and I would like to continue doing so in the future.

Understanding the Students

Prior to reflecting my experience in attempting to understand the students, it is essential for me to explain the nature of the academic skills courses in both Malaysia and the United Kingdom to provide the context for the opportunities and challenges that I faced.

In Malaysia, I taught academic skills as a part of English as an Academic Purposes (EAP) course that was compulsory for the students. This means that I met the students on a weekly basis for at least three months. Within that duration, I was able to develop a relationship with the students and learn about their abilities. I took time to understand and get to know my students as suggested by Mahan and Stein (2014) about teachers taking their time to understand learners. As such, I could keep on adapting the coming lessons to suit the students' abilities, progress and backgrounds. This is not the case in my teaching in the United Kingdom. The academic courses that I have taught here stand on its own as an optional learning support that students have access to. Students choose which courses they want to attend for their skills development. There is no pass or fail, but students will receive a participation certificate that is useful for future employment. If the students miss the course that they have booked for three times, they would be banned from joining future courses for that particular term.

Now I would like to relate the context explained to the opportunities and challenges I experienced regarding student engagement. Student engagement is twofold – both teachers and students are responsible for increasing student engagement. I will discuss both.

A major difference is that my students in Malaysia *had* to learn the academic skills as a course requirement, while my students in the United Kingdom choose to attend the academic courses because they *want* to. This difference is related to the intentions of the students. As explained by Bryan (2015), students' intentions in learning will determine whether they have a deep or surface approach to learning and assessment. Students have a deep approach when they aim towards understanding lessons. If they aim to reproduce material for exam purposes, then the learning is categorised as a surface approach. Nonetheless, it is not my intention to say that the existence of assessment will solely determine students' intentions. That would be too simplistic. My point here is, my students in the United Kingdom attended the courses because they saw the relevance of learning particular skills. Because there was no assessment at all, I am confident to say that these students' intentions were to learn and apply the skills in their academic or general life. These students were aware of how the courses would help them in self-development, which means their motivation to learning comes from within – this is what is called intrinsic motivation.

The fact that my UK students attended the courses showed that they were motivated and ready to learn. Biggs and Tang (2007) emphasise that for students to be engaged in tasks, they need to expect success. They also mentioned that good teaching should focus on motivation as the outcome of learning, not as a precondition. As these UK students had an intrinsic motivation in learning, my role here was to keep them motivated and engaged throughout the lesson. Again, this is related to 'the maintenance' (see Whitaker et al., 2018). At this point, I would like to stress once more on the importance of outcome-based learning (see Biggs & Tang, 2007). At the onset of any course, it is important that learning outcomes are communicated and explained to the students so that they could assess their own learning.

It seemed that I would have an easy job in teaching students that were intrinsically motivated to learn. However, I would like to kindly remind that the course I taught were open to students from any level and field of study. I would have a diverse set of undergraduates and postgraduates from the law school, medical school, physics department and humanities department – just to name a few. This was where the challenges came. I had to increase and maintain student engagement for a diverse set of students that I had just met. The duration for each course that I taught was two hours. Since I did not have the time to get to know the students in depth, I felt that maintaining engagement with students I knew little about was a challenge. From my teaching experiences in Malaysia, I was better acquainted with my students and was able to maintain student engagement because I had time to get to know them first. I could see that this relationship was important for engagement. I have to admit that it was too ambitious for me to engage all students. What important is that I understand the process of learning and how those processes could be interpreted into creating an inclusive lesson.

The learning stages are best explained using the Structured of the Observed Learning Outcome (SOLO) taxonomy illustrated in Figure 4.1.

Biggs' (n.d.) description of the taxonomy is self-explained. 'At first we pick up only one or few aspects of the task (unistructural), then several aspects

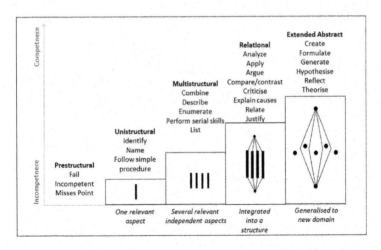

Figure 4.1 The SOLO (structured of the observed learning outcome) (adapted from Biggs, n.d.)

but they are unrelated (multistructural), then we learn how to integrate them into a whole (relational), and finally, we are able to generalise that whole to as yet, untaught applications (extended abstract)'. How I put this taxonomy into practice was by guiding the students throughout the process of understanding and learning. I started by introducing the skill in general, what it compassed and then explored with them how the new skill could be applied in their context and field of study. I referred to Moon's (2013) model of depth of learning for this approach. Depth of learning consists of five stages: (1) noticing; (2) making sense; (3) making meaning; (4) working with meaning and (5) transformative learning. It is important for me to make the students think about their plans in practising the skills.

Although the courses I taught were pre-designed, I had the freedom to make adjustments based on the students' individual needs as suggested by the Universal Design for Learning (UDL). The UDL framework states that teaching goals, methods and materials could be customised to meet individual needs as a mean to create an inclusive learning environment. UDL comes in handy when teaching groups of students that are culturally diverse – which was my case. After teaching a few courses, I realised that I needed to make some minor changes to the pre-designed course. I could not change the main content, but I worked around the content and included additional activities by considering students' field of studies as shared when they introduced themselves. I consistently checked students' understanding by providing opportunities for discussion and keeping the interaction open. When necessary, I made a prompt decision to leave out activities that were not relevant to the group of students that I taught. For examples, preparing for and delivering presentation skills were taught in separate workshops. However, there was a time when I taught a small group of students, fewer than ten students, all of them wanted to learn both skills in that particular workshop. Based on the students' reasons of coming to the workshops, I chose only important and relevant activities so that I could cover the contents of two workshops in one.

Other than learning to be flexible with my teaching, there was something new that I learned as a result of diversity and cultural differences. Diversity is defined as 'differences of experience, interest, orientation to the world, values, dispositions, sensibilities, social languages and discourses' (Cope & Kalantzis, 2009, p. 173). A contrasting culture I have noticed between Malaysia and the United Kingdom is the relationship between teachers and students.

In Malaysia, it is a norm for teachers to develop a close relationship with the students. Although it is an individual's choice, it is not uncommon to see teachers and students share their personal mobile phone numbers to ease communication – mostly on assignments. Other examples of this close relationship are teachers and students eating out in groups, students visiting teachers' houses during festival celebrations and being friends on social media. This is not allowed in the United Kingdom. The education system in the United Kingdom takes the personal-professional boundary seriously as part of safeguarding. The UK Education Act (2002) limits the relationship between teacher and pupils (and young people) to safeguard young people and protect teachers from any allegations. As such, I only share my email address when needed and only if I wanted to. If there was time, I would entertain students' questions after each lesson. Otherwise, I encouraged students to email me and if there was any need for a face-to-face meeting, it was done only at a cafe on campus within my working hours.

Realising that my students came from various parts of the world, I learned to appreciate different opinions. The interaction I had with my students was actually a way to build a relationship with people across cultures and to develop empathetic intercultural viewpoints (Hepple, 2014). Having a 'sympathetic imagination' allows me to see other cultures as sharing of problems and possibilities (Nussbaum, 1997). The experience of having this kind of discussion has made me challenge my own perceptions of interculturality. Bias is something humans are grown with, but I have learned that I could empower myself with knowledge to control and minimise bias. I have learned to acknowledge differences and recognise uniqueness. I have learned to focus on commonalities and embrace differences.

Finding Meaning in My Experience

I would like to conclude this chapter by relating my experience, regardless in Malaysia or the UK context, to the four scholarships proposed by Boyer (1990) in Figure 4.2. Boyer (1990) explained academic activities as a cycle

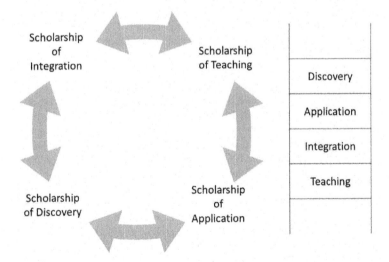

Figure 4.2 Depiction of Boyer's (1990) scholarships by Lea and Purcell (2015).

that repeats the four scholarships – discovery, application, integration and teaching. As an academic, this cycle accurately represents my teaching experience. Picking up each step in Boyer's model, I will explain how I intend to continue the learning process as an educator. First, as regards the scholarship of teaching, this is mainly about making an effort to understand what happens beyond the act of teaching itself. This involves numerous theories, approaches and concepts. For example, pedagogy, classroom management, student behaviour and student engagement. By understanding the literature, I will be able to decide which teaching strategies, activities and approaches suit the students. Second, the scholarship of application in which I apply my knowledge and skills in teaching. This step is related to the scholarship of discovery as applying the knowledge into practice allows me to discover which method works, and which does not. Finally, the scholarship of integration is about blending the literature, the discovery and the teaching I have had to improve the teaching and learning process continuously.

Having said this, the opportunities and challenges I faced in both countries are of invaluable experience. What important in the process is that I reflect on the experiences, as being reflective makes me aware of my teaching approach, the rationality of why I do what I do and how I could apply those experiences for future teaching, regardless of where I teach.

References

Biggs, J. (n.d.). *SOLO taxonomy*. Retrieved June 7, 2020, from www.johnbiggs.com. au/academic/solo-taxonomy/

Biggs, J., & Tang, C. (2007). *Teaching for quality learning at university* (3rd ed.). SRHE and Open University Press.

Boyer, E. L. (1990). *Scholarship reconsidered: Priorities for the professoriate*. Princeton University Press: Carnegie Foundation for the Advancement of Teaching.

Bryan, B. (2015). Enhancing student learning. In J. Lea (Ed.), *Enhancing learning and teaching in higher education: Engaging with the dimensions of practice*. McGraw-Hill Education.

Cope, B., & Kalantzis, M. (2009). "Multiliteracies": New literacies, new learning. *Pedagogies: An International Journal, 4*(3), 164–195.

Current Population Estimates. (2022). *Department of statistics Malaysia*. Retrieved January 12, 2023, from www.dosm.gov.my/v1/index.php?r=column/pdfPrev&id=dTZXanV6UUdyUEQ0SHNWOVhpSXNMUT09#:~:text=The%20total%20population%20of%20Malaysia,to%202.4%20million%20(2022)

The UK Education Act (2002). Retrieved June 7, 2020, from www.legislation.gov.uk/ukpga/2002/32/contents

Emmer, E. T., & Sabornie, E. J. (2015). *Handbook of classroom management* (2nd ed.). Routledge, Taylor & Francis Group.

Hamre, B. K., Pianta, R. C., Downer, J. T., & Mashburn, A. J. (2008). Teachers' perceptions of conflict with young students: Looking beyond problem behaviours. *Social Development, 17*, 115–136. https://doi.org/10.1111/j.1467–9507.2007.00418.x

Hepple, E. (2014). Developing cosmopolitan professional identities: Engaging Australian and Hong Kong trainee teachers. In intercultural conversations. In N. Haydari & P. Holmes (Eds.), *Case studies in intercultural dialogue* (pp. 87–102). Kendall Hunt Publishing.

HE Student Enrolments by Domicile. (2022). *Where do HE students come from?* Retrieved January 12, 2023, from www.hesa.ac.uk/data-and-analysis/students/where-from

Lea, J., & Purcell, N. (2015). Introduction: The scholarship of teaching and learning, the Higher Education Academy, and the UK professional standards framework. In J. Lea (Ed.), *Enhancing learning and teaching in higher education: Engaging with the dimensions of practice.* McGraw-Hill Education.

Mahan, J. D., & Stein, D. S. (2014). Teaching adults-best practices that leverage the emerging understanding of the neurobiology of learning. *Current Problems in Pediatric and Adolescent Health Care, 44,* 141–149.

Moon, J. A. (2013). *Reflection in learning and professional development: Theory and practice.* Taylor and Francis.

Nussbaum, M. C. (1997). *Cultivating humanity: A classical defense of reform in liberal education.* Harvard University Press.

Quick Facts 2021: Malaysian Educational Statistics. (2021). *Educational planning and research division.* Retrieved January 12, 2023, from www.moe.gov.my/menumedia/media-cetak/penerbitan/quick-facts/4589-quick-facts-2021/file

Quigley, A. (2016). *The confident teacher: Developing successful habits of mind, body and pedagogy.* Routledge.

Spencer-Oatey, H. (2008). *Culturally speaking: Culture, communication and politeness theory* (2nd ed.). Continuum.

Spencer-Oatey, H., & Kadar, D. Z. (2021). *Intercultural politeness: Managing relations across cultures.* Cambridge University Press.

Whitaker, T., Good, M. W., & Whitaker, K. (2018). *Classroom management from the ground up* (1st ed.). Routledge.

5 Teachers' Beliefs and Opportunities in Light of the Curriculum Reform in Malaysian Classrooms

Tun, Nadia, and Khairuddin, Zurina

Introduction

The Malaysian education system, like many other developing countries, is steered towards producing holistic students and teachers. In the Malaysian context, holistic is interpreted as being 'knowledgeable and proficient, possessing high moral standard, and capable of contributing to the betterment of family, society and country' (MoE Malaysia, 2013, pp. E–4). One of the efforts implemented by the Ministry of Education (MoE) is establishing the National Education Philosophy (NEP) which emphasises the ongoing effort towards the development of an individual's potential in a holistic manner – 'intellectually, spiritually, emotionally and physically' (MoE Malaysia, 2015, pp. 2–2). The MoE also enriches its national curriculum by integrating a set of skills and competencies, namely 'knowledge, thinking skills, leadership skills, bilingual proficiency, ethics and spirituality and national identity' (MoE Malaysia, 2013, pp. 2–6). These skills need to be mastered by Malaysian students in this competitive world. It is believed that these skills can produce Malaysians who are 'balanced, resilient, inquisitive, patriotic, critical thinkers, and equipped' with basic competencies required in the 21st century (MoE Malaysia, 2013, pp. 2–6). In line with the notion mentioned earlier, we believe there is an urge for the education system as well as teacher roles to be modernised and aligned with the demands in creating knowledge-based economies (OECD, 2009). Nonetheless, it is a common opinion that the Malaysian education system heavily focuses on assessing students' through centralised public examination and rote learning (Effandi & Zanatun, 2007; Gopala, Roszainora Setia et al., 2014; Alla Baksh et al., 2016) rather than through their skills and competencies.

Hence, there is a great emphasis on the learning output rather than its process. As those who have been in the system, we experienced this for years. For example, in primary and secondary schools, we were drilled into answering past exam questions to get good grades for the centralised exams rather than being taught how to scaffold understanding upon the context of the subject matter. Teachers were instructed by the school authority to provide extra

DOI: 10.4324/9781003374190-5

classes outside of school hours which included evenings and weekends. We also experienced class streaming, referring to when those who did not perform well in the centralised exams would be placed in the low academic achiever classes and vice versa. This kind of environment left soft skills (e.g. communicative ability, critical thinking), that we should have developed during schooling years, neglected. This is contrary to what is stated in the NEP about holistic education, and it explains the unsatisfactory record of achievements (below average) among Malaysian students in international assessments like the Programme for International Student Assessment (PISA) (Economic Planning Unit, 2015). The outcomes of this assessment show that Malaysian students lack knowledge application and reasoning skills. The lack of soft skills has also impacted the Malaysian graduates' employability. This is evident when employers and industry leaders revealed that they were concerned about the lack of 'higher-order thinking skills, such as problem-solving and creative thinking, and the level of graduates' English proficiency' (MoE Malaysia, 2013, pp. 3–15). Thus, we believe that curriculum reform ought to start from the bottom (school context), where the focus should be on the improvement of school leadership, teachers' teaching practices, and students' achievement. The most important part of these improvements is the role of teachers who can be the agent of change of the reform and the driving force in producing holistic citizens as stated in the NEP (Wallin, 2003).

What we experienced as a student was not uncommon and many, like us, realised the shortcomings of the existing educational system in Malaysia. Thus, in 2011, an educational reform took place in both primary and secondary schools in Malaysia to instigate a holistic and high-quality education of international standards in classroom learning (MoE Malaysia, 2013). The reform occurred after the MoE comprehensively reviewed its system in developing a newly improvised and enhanced national curriculum. As stated by the MoE Malaysia (2013), the reformation was initiated to meet the needs of international education standards and revisit its NEP in preparing and producing Malaysian students who possess higher order thinking skills (HOTS) and the ability to implement and exhibit 'reasoning, creativity and innovation' skills (MoE Malaysia, 2013, pp. 3–4). The curriculum policy clearly states that HOTS should now be inculcated in the curriculum and emphasised in the classroom through teaching and learning activities – in the form of reasoning, inquiry learning and problem solving – and in doing so, pupils are given the power and responsibility to manage their own learning (MoE Malaysia, 2013). Considering what Malaysian students experienced prior to the reform, on paper, this newly developed curriculum is considerably more comprehensive and balanced. We believe it can be beneficial not only to educators and students but also to industry players. From our viewpoint, what makes this reform more appealing is the changes in how the national examinations measure the students' ability – from merely testing knowledge and understanding to determining the extent of the students' HOTS (MoE Malaysia, 2013).

Even though things seemed promising with the curriculum reform, teachers' readiness remains one of the main concerns. As teachers ourselves, we foresee the reform would require a lot of commitment and sacrifices. As mentioned earlier, teachers were viewed as the key players in the reform, and as such could also be the barriers to the reform's success if they were not willing to renegotiate their existing beliefs on issues involving teaching and learning. For the reform to take place, some modifications had to be made to their existing – in particular the obsolete and traditional – classroom instructional practices. As teachers, we believe the whole idea of the reform demanded some negotiation and modifications on teachers' beliefs and attitudes if they were to fit the newly revised content of the curriculum. This is because the content of the curriculum reform may influence the norm of their existing, current classroom practices (more on teachers' beliefs and classroom practices in Elbaz, 1983; Burns, 1992; Borg, 2003).

In short, teachers' perceptions and behaviours are deeply rooted in their beliefs on teaching and learning. This is why we perceive teachers' beliefs and attitude as the main drivers of an effective curriculum reform. To gain more understanding of this notion, we have decided to present in this chapter an in-depth reflection on teachers' beliefs and opportunities in light of the curriculum reform. We find it important to revisit and acknowledge the teachers' beliefs and opportunities so that we are able to see what it really takes for a curriculum reform to succeed.

The Malaysian Education System

The roles of teachers in the global education context have been under the spotlight due to many reasons. One of them is the rising concerns on the outdated education mainstream at present where schools are still regarded as 19th-century institutions. This also leads to the failure of teachers' pedagogical approach in producing updated knowledge for the workforce (Robertson, 2005). The impact of neoliberal policies on teachers that includes 'intensification, role overload, de-professionalisation and student behaviour' is also a noteworthy point in highlighting the role of teachers in today's world (Macbeath, 2012). These policies have caused teaching to be an undesirable profession in some parts of the world including Malaysia (Macbeath, 2012). In Malaysia, misconceptions about teachers' competencies have led to negative remarks on the profession itself, thus requiring some moral uplifting (Siti Suriani, 2007). Malaysian graduates have been found to perceive this career as a forced, last option for when they could not find or secure their desired jobs (reference). This circumstance has led to an increased number of non-option teachers who do not possess a degree in education.

A study suggests that the success and failure of an educational reform are closely associated with the roles of teachers (Zeichner & Ndimande, 2008). Believing this is true, we would like to think that any pedagogical approaches in teaching and learning predominantly fall into the hands of teachers in delivering classroom instructions (Yap, 2004; Ng et al., 2005; Yew Tee et al., 2018). While this is comforting for us as teachers, studies have indicated that many teachers in Malaysia may have not played their roles well, especially in providing a constructive and engaging learning environment for students. For example, a study conducted by the MoE (2013) in 41 schools in Malaysia revealed that 50% of the lessons delivered by teachers were insufficient in engaging the students' participation. The content was delivered through non-interactive lectures and the emphasis was merely on memorising and recalling facts, which mainly prepared the students to sit for summative assessments instead of promoting HOTS and communication skills (Economic Planning Unit, 2015) as desired in the curriculum reform. This study also echoes a study conducted by Yew Tee et al. (2018) in which students were found to be passively engaged in learning because learning activities conducted were mostly teacher-centred, facts- and procedures-driven, and applied minimal level of HOTS.

The findings of both studies above describe the current situation of teaching and learning approaches in Malaysia that were developed based upon the practice of teacher-centredness and rote learning. Activities such as 'drilling, memorization, choral reading, and teachers asking questions' are widely used in demonstrating certain amounts of knowledge (Richard & Rodgers, 2001, p. 5). Utilising too many of these approaches could affect the students' learning and they will likely become less inquisitive and rarely share opinions (Effandi & Zanatun, 2007). In addressing the issues raised, the new curriculum was introduced by the Ministry of Education which aims to produce students who possess HOTS, actively engage in building new knowledge and concepts based on their schemata, and are able to apply the knowledge and skills beyond the academic context (MoE Malaysia, 2013; Zamri, 2016). This would require teachers to integrate the constructivism approach in their teaching, thus giving the students more opportunities to engage in problem solving and to be exposed to more student-centred activities (OECD, 2009).

While the student-centred approach is seen as a better form of the pedagogical approach due to its power dynamic distribution between the students and teachers, we believe the combination of student- and teacher-centred approaches can be complementary in the teaching and learning process. In fact, this combination can enhance and maximise both teachers' and students' learning experiences when applied in appropriate learning contexts using the right materials (Emaliana, 2017). For example, our class consists of students with different levels of proficiency. As observant teachers, we can usually adapt and modify our teaching instructions and practices according to the atmosphere of the class. If the class seems quiet or unengaged, we often use more structured, teacher-centred instructions to help students to familiarise themselves with the lesson. This would help students with lower level of proficiency too. As students become more engaged with the lesson and come closer to meeting the learning objectives, we will start giving them less structured and more complex instructions to follow. This will allow them to have some freedom in class and to bring whatever they have to the table. We believe that exercising a balanced power dynamic in the teacher-student relationship could empower our roles as teachers and most importantly, students in their own, thus providing a positive and meaningful classroom experience for both.

Malaysian Teacher Education

Malaysia has been gearing its economic growth towards an increased and enhanced productivity, and human capital development (PEMANDU, 2010). To achieve such goals, a highly skilled, creative and innovative workforce is in great demand, thus requiring teachers' pedagogical approaches and students' learning experiences to be modified and flexible. These modifications and flexibilities are crucial in developing skills befitting the current intellectual and social needs among Malaysians (UNESCO, 2015). Consequently, the modifications and flexibilities can be projected onto the education system effectively if we are able to produce 'knowledgeable, resilient and quality' educators (Jala, 2010). However, going through such a process can be challenging, not only for policy makers, but also to school administrators, students, and the educators, whom is considered as the agents of change. Reflecting on our own experience, developing such attributes in students can be challenging because knowledge is complex and global. Hence, a good quality in teacher training programmes is required to fulfil the need to develop such students. As educators, we believe that any educational reform should not only look at the students' attainment. In implementing the reform, one should also consider how the quality and good attributes of teachers can be significantly reflected and articulated in the teachers' standards that should be made available within teacher training programmes.

In Malaysia, teacher training colleges and some universities (public or private) are responsible in providing pre-service teacher education to student teachers (Hazri et al., 2011). The entry requirements and duration of the studies vary depending on the courses offered by the respective institutions or universities. Teacher education programmes in Malaysia focus mainly on getting student teachers to acquire a set of generic teaching skills, such as preparing lesson plans for teaching, managing classrooms appropriately and possessing instructional skills which include drilling and praising. The curriculum designed for the teacher education programme is meant to be holistic and balanced and should be driven by knowledge, skills and values. It is tailored to be 'outcome-based, coherent, spiral, holistic, practical and contextual' (Hazri et al., 2011). This aligns with what is envisioned by the Malaysian Qualifying Framework (MQF) where the elements mentioned are consistent with 21st-century skills. Hence, in producing future educators with such attributes, curriculum, co-curriculum activities and Teacher Character Building Course are also embedded in the training programme (Phoi & Peng, 2012). The nature of the programme allowed student teachers to experience real classroom practices first hand. Student teachers also had to attend lectures, complete practical tasks and coursework, and sit for examinations in order to complete training. To gain an exposure of the school cultures, student teachers had to undergo school-based experience programmes and teaching practicum.

The teacher training programme described earlier, although based on our own account, is generally the standard practice across teacher training colleges in Malaysia. The programme is outlined using the Malaysian Teacher Standard (MTS) which specifies the high competency teacher standards around four domains: 'professional knowledge and skills; personal characteristics; professional or personal ethical values; and professional development and lifelong learning' (SEAMEO INNOTECH, 2010). The standards are guidelines for teachers in that they outline how teachers can develop their teaching skills in assisting students to achieve their learning outcomes and assessing students at a higher level of thinking through problem solving and decision making (Zakaria, 2000; Hussin, 2002). This MTS is aimed to improve our quality as teachers and the quality of our pedagogical practices and elevate our status. This is also portrayed in other countries like South Africa, Singapore, the United Kingdom and the United States (Westbrook, 2017).

The objectives of the MTS and the role of the MTS in guiding teachers are evidently clear and well-established. However, the MTS does not address the challenges teacher educators have to face in producing qualified teachers. In fact, as proposed by Swee (2012), teacher educators are encouraged to renegotiate the deep-rooted beliefs, values, and biased views that student teachers have obtained from their own school experiences which usually lead to misconceptions regarding the teaching profession. We believe teacher educators need to fill in the gap between what is articulated in the MTS and what the reality serves in today's Malaysian teaching and learning environment. Along with these, teacher educators have to focus on the actual training of teachers itself, which in our opinion can be both thought-provoking and exhausting.

From a different perspective, Phoi and Peng (2012) indicated in their research that student teachers found it challenging to be in the training programme. The student teachers were unsure if they were being trained to design meaningful learning activities for pedagogical purposes throughout the training programme. They also had difficulties in putting into practice the theoretical knowledge specifically in their specialised field. Apart from this, the student teachers also stated that the programme did not train them to synthesise information from multiple relevant sources to bridge their understanding of theory and practice. Finally, the student teachers also shared that they struggled to identify and explain the procedures of relevant assessment in their respective fields. The grievances reported earlier are similar to what we encountered when we were student teachers. Reflecting on our own experiences, despite going through a series of mock teaching presentations and being presented with a heavy load of theoretical and pedagogical knowledge in teaching and learning, it was difficult to picture how teaching practicum at school would look like.

The challenges discussed earlier demonstrate that there is a mismatch between the teacher training programmes, the NEP and the teacher education philosophy. This mismatch needs to be addressed in order to produce Malaysian teachers who are competent, practical, skilled, responsible and ethical (Phoi & Peng, 2012). In reducing the challenges faced by student teachers due to the lack of training (Mat Yusoff et al., 2016), more intensive and comprehensive teacher training programmes should be provided to ensure student teachers have what it takes to be the catalysts of the educational reform. Thus, in making this a success, teacher educators should be provided with updated and/or enhanced Continuing Professional Development (CPD). CPD would help to develop and enhance their pedagogical content knowledge and skills to ensure the teachers are consistently updated with the latest and relevant teaching practices.

Teachers' Beliefs and Possible Opportunities

Looking back at what we have described about the Malaysian education system and teacher education, we believe Malaysian teachers have the tendency to practice only the teacher-centred approach in the classroom. We personally experienced this when we were student teachers and when we first started our career in the teaching profession. Thus, in order to successfully align with the needs of the reform, the majority of the teachers may need to go through some transformation if they are to produce students who are able to compete in a 'knowledge-based' economy. This transformation requires some adaptations and adjustments in terms of teachers' instructional and pedagogical approaches in the classrooms. This includes changing the forms of assessment (Resnick & Resnick, 1991; Messick, 1994) and activities conducted in the classrooms. The best example of transformation, in relation to the new classroom practices that aligns with the new curriculum, is a combination of student-centred and teacher-centred learning approaches. However, as we have described earlier, this is not commonly practiced by teachers, nor by student teachers in teacher training colleges (Azhar, 2012; Mat Yusoff et al., 2016).

Hence, we believe that as teachers, we should be well-prepared before the transformation of the revised curriculum takes place. One of the important elements to look at is our existing beliefs of what constitutes teaching and learning in the classroom context. This belief or cognition should focus on what we 'know, believe and think' (Borg, 2003). This cognition acts as an 'intel' in informing us beforehand to what extent we implement our teaching practices in line with our cognition (Beach, 1994). In this case, we, as teachers, should be more flexible and accepting of new or different pedagogical approaches alongside any educational reform.

Our proposition may sound too simplistic. However, we believe that the renegotiation and flexibility of one's belief and attitude are crucial. This includes getting ourselves to become more accepting, committed, and passionate before the education takes place (Guskey, 2002). In addition, our pedagogical beliefs significantly influence our decision-making regarding teaching approaches and thus classroom practices. (Borg, 2003; Breen et al., 2003; Farrel & Benisi, 2013). Therefore, we strongly believe that any educational reform meant for an improved education standard should offer us continuous, comprehensive and high-quality professional development trainings. These trainings should focus on the modification of 'professional practices, beliefs and understanding of, in most cases, the students' learning attainment' (Guskey, 2002).

To reiterate, changing teachers' beliefs is crucial and challenging because a belief is 'deeply engraved and difficult to change' (Guskey, 2002). Nevertheless, we know this is possible and applicable if we do it properly and relentlessly. Guskey (2002) has outlined a model of teacher change with regard to beliefs, attitudes, and perceptions (see Figure 5.1).

Guskey's model above shows how beliefs and attitudes can change after experiencing professional development. This change can later transform classroom practices. The change in classroom practices leads to the change in the student learning outcome. This means that the change in students' attainment is influenced by the modifications we make on our instructional approaches, teaching methods and classroom assessment. According to Guskey (2002), change is seen as an experience-based learning process for teachers. A noteworthy point highlighted in Guskey's model is that this kind of change experienced by teachers, which in this context refers to teachers' classroom practices and students' learning outcome, are said to influence the teachers' belief and attitudes towards teaching and learning in the classroom (Guskey, 2002). In short, if we are exposed to appropriate and sufficient continuous professional development trainings, we should be ready and able to adapt or adopt what we have learned or experienced into our existing classroom practices. The change in our practices would impact the students' learning attainment, and their existing belief and attitudes towards what constitutes teaching and learning.

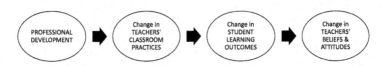

Figure 5.1 Guskey's teacher model of change

On the basis of Guskey's model, we believe the MoE should implement a more systematic and organised effort, such as providing more comprehensive and sufficient CPD to us, the teachers, to generate the change in our classroom practices, attitudes and beliefs, thus producing students' learning outcomes that are in tandem with the new curriculum. The MoE could provide more series of CPD programmes for teachers like us (Talib et al., 2014; Mat Yusoff et al., 2016). These CPD programmes could be organised to guide us on the implementation of the curriculum reform. Comprehensive and appropriate trainings could enhance our interest and thus increase enthusiasm in regard to attitudes, knowledge and skills towards the reform (Jaba, 2013). This will indirectly aid us in renegotiating our beliefs which may result in the changes of our classroom teaching practices and the students' learning outcomes. To date, however, CPD trainings addressing curriculum reforms are scarce. Many teachers, as reported by Mohd Asari (2013), demanded for these curriculum-reform related trainings to be carried out regularly and continuously.

While it was enriching to have various levels of training, many of the sessions conducted did not provide comprehensive and sufficient trainings for us to prepare ourselves for the reform and this has led to the poor quality of teacher training (Mat Yusoff et al., 2016). Most of these teacher training programmes revolve around lectures and briefings that emphasise one-way communication instead of two-way, and lack hands-on activities which result in the deterioration of teachers' interest towards the respective subject content (Mat Yusoff et al., 2016). Numerous studies have also confirmed that teachers perceived the training to be only satisfactory (see Hassan et al., 2006; Moidunny, 2009). Reflecting on our own experiences, the training programmes paid too much attention to the theoretical parts of the reform whilst the critical and real issues emerging in the implementation process of the reform were not acknowledged (Azhar, 2012). Therefore, we believe that facilitators who are involved in the training should be more proactive in providing engaging activities. They should also encourage participants (student teachers) to engage actively throughout the learning process and often ask them their opinions and views regarding the implementation of the reform with regard to the appropriateness of the targeted learning content.

Apart from the issues above, many teachers are often uncertain of their roles in implementing the new curriculum (Majid, 2011) despite a number of courses being available to them (Vethamani, 2011; Yusof Petras et al., 2012). Some were reported to be struggling in implementing new assessments (Sobri, 2011; Lee, 2012) because they were not provided with proper training on how to carry out the newly revised assessment in the classroom (Malakolunthu & Kwan, 2010). Apart from non-existent training, the struggle is also rooted in 'insufficient guidelines provided by the MoE, lack of external monitoring on the implementation in school, time constraints, increased teacher workload and poor teacher knowledge-base' (Malakolunthu & Kwan, 2010; Talib et al., 2014). Studies investigating teachers' implementation of new initiatives (see

Tobin & Lamaster, 1995; McRobbie & Tobin, 1995) indicate that teachers have to renegotiate their belief system. This occurs when there is a mismatch between the concepts of curricular innovation and teachers' beliefs. This renegotiation may be troublesome to teachers and to a certain extent, may lead to teachers feeling inferior, thus affecting their confidence in their own abilities and roles (Shanusi, 2007). This situation is very much similar to what we and other teachers in Malaysia have been experiencing during the curriculum reform.

In response to all the issues described earlier, as teachers, we need to prepare ourselves by participating in comprehensive and adequate trainings so as to increase and enhance our competency. Other than ensuring comprehensive understanding to the newly developed teaching practices, we should also stay committed and interested throughout our endeavours to fulfil the objectives of the educational reform. This is because teachers can effectively engage and perform well in any educational reform if they fully grasp the concept to be embedded and modified in classroom learning (Torrance, 1995). Therefore, adequate and proper teacher training including a continuous series of effective CPD programmes should be carried out to guide and help teachers develop the beliefs, knowledge and skills congruent with what is required in implementing the curriculum reform.

Developing Teacher's Beliefs through Effective CPD Programmes

In Malaysia, pre-service and in-service teachers' professional development courses are managed by the Teacher Education Division (TED). Osman and Kassim (2013) highlight that the training module provided by the division often require teachers to attend courses that expose them to "prescriptive modules that give precise instruction to teachers on the 'what' and 'how' to teach specific subjects and content." They also point out how such trainings limit teachers' creativity and freedom to exercise their autonomy in learning. Consequently, teachers become more dependent, less creative and are prone to be reluctance in taking the risks to modify their teachings practices to best suit their students' learning. Hence, scholars suggest that effective CPD programmes should include active learning, a strong content focus, coherence, a reasonable time frame and collective participation (Garet et al., 2001; Desimone, 2009; Luft & Hewson, 2014). Active learning in CPD allows us to observe our colleagues, apply what we have learned and get feedback from others, review and evaluate students' tasks, lead and get actively involved in discussions, implement new knowledge into teaching or participate in activities as students (Garet et al., 2001; Heller et al., 2012). In addition, content focus should be embedded into CPD programmes where the focus is not only on increasing and enhancing our knowledge but also on driving to improve teaching practices (Garet et al., 2001; Kennedy, 2005;

Desimone, 2009). Hence, it is crucial for us to master this pedagogical content knowledge for better quality of instruction and student achievement (Darling-Hammond, 1999).

Coherence is also a vital element in structuring effective CPD programmes. Coherence, in this context, relates to how CPD programmes could be integrated into our learning. Activities implemented should guide and inform us to identify and acknowledge the challenges faced in classrooms, hence helping to plan and implement interventions where necessary (Ottoson, 1997). In carrying out new practices, mentoring and coaching sessions should be made available to teachers (Smith & Ingersoll, 2004; Luft et al., 2011; Grierson & Woloshyn, 2013). This would allow teachers to get access for individualised feedback that are tailored to their needs and classroom context. Mentoring and coaching could be a great support system in informing teachers of any significant modifications to be applied to existing practices (Grierson & Woloshyn, 2013).

In terms of the duration of CPD programmes, researchers agreed that the longer the duration, the more effective it is in changing our practices (Porter et al., 2000; Banilower et al., 2007; Gerard et al., 2011). According to Porter et al. (2000), a longer period of CPD can lead one to more active learning, coherence, and to be more content-focused in comparison to shorter programmes. A study showed that professional development programmes that last from six to 12 months with an average of 30–100 hours can have a positive and significant impact on student learning attainment (Wei et al., 2010). On the other hand, brief, one-off programmes have less or little effect on our professional growth or comprehension (Loucks-Horsley & Matsumoto, 1999; Spillane, 2002; Pianta, 2011). Hence, it might not have a significant impact on the students' learning (Wei et al., 2010).

A collective participation in CPD programmes also encourages us within the same school, department, subject or grade to communicate and discuss with each other (Porter et al., 2000; Desimone, 2009). Working collaboratively allows us to discuss curricular changes more effectively, thus initiating a professional learning community that can motivate us to consistently improve our practices (Loucks-Horsley & Matsumoto, 1999; Porter et al., 2000; Borko, 2004).

The elements presented earlier are parts of the attributes and conditions of CPD programmes believed to be the most effective in encouraging teacher change and/or impacting student learning attainment (Garet et al., 2001; Knapp, 2003; Borko, 2004). Since the implementation of curriculum reform in Malaysia is delivered top down, from government and policy makers, it is crucial to consider the attributes or elements of effective CPD programmes as a common standard to be set for both the policy makers and practitioners. This would guide and allow them to make the relevant changes for the betterment of teachers' quality performance.

Conclusion

The curriculum reform introduced by the Ministry of Education is believed to be a stepping stone and part of the effort to enhance and increase the quality of student's attainment. However, we believe the objectives of the reform may not be fulfilled if we, the teachers, do not fully comprehend its notion and are not fully equipped with the appropriate knowledge and skills (Chapman & Snyder, 2000; Stillman, 2001). Hence, we should be provided with continuous, adequate and quality teacher training programmes which include active learning, a strong content focus, coherence, a reasonable time frame, and collective participation. Teachers or educators who are unprepared might find themselves struggling in adapting to any newly introduced educational system for they have to learn new skills (or modify the existing ones), and adjust to new or enhanced forms of assessment and instructional practices. The possibility of applying or implementing the new curriculum lies upon our openness, acceptance, and flexibility towards existing and new pedagogies; and our willingness to adjust or be more flexible in negotiating and/or renegotiating our own beliefs in teaching and in the students' learning. We firmly believe that in order for a reform to take place effectively, the content of the curriculum and teachers' competencies should align. These competencies can be achieved if we, as teachers, possess positive beliefs, perceptions and have the required knowledge of the content of the reform which involve many changes in different stages.

References

Alla Baksh, M. A., Mohd Sallehhudin, A. A., Tayeb, Y. A., & Norhaslinda, H. (2016). Washback effect of school-based English language assessment: A case-study on students' perceptions. *Pertanika Journal of Social Sciences & Humanities, 24*(3), 1069–1086.

Azhar, R. (2012). *Pentaksiran Berasaskan sekolah: Pelaksanaan dan cabaran* (The post-modern perspective on educational needs). http://cikguazharrodzi.blogspot.co.uk/2012/06/pentaksiran-berasaskan-sekolah.html

Banilower, E. R., Heck, D. J., & Weiss, I. R. (2007). Can professional development make the vision of the standards a reality? The impact of the national science foundation's local systemic change through teacher enhancement initiative. *Journal of Research on Science Teaching, 44*, 375–395.

Beach, S. A. (1994). Teachers' theories and classroom practice: Beliefs, knowledge, or context? *Reading Psychology, 3*(15), 189–196.

Borg, S. (2003). Teacher cognition in language teaching: A review of research on what language teachers think, know, believe, and do. *Language Teaching, 36*(2), 81–109. https://doi.org/10.1017/S0261444803001903

Borko, H. (2004). Professional development and teacher learning: Mapping the terrain. *Educational Researcher, 8*(33), 3–15.

Breen, M. P., Hird, B., Milton, M., Oliver, R., & Thwaite, A. (2003). Making sense of language teaching: Teachers' principles and classroom practices. *Applied Linguistics, 22*(4), 470–401. https://doi.org/10.1093/applin/22.4.470

Burns, A. (1992). Teacher belief and their influence on classroom practice. *Prospect, 7*, 56–66.

Chapman, D. W., & Snyder, C. W. (2000). Can high stakes national testing improve instruction: Reexamining conventional wisdom. *International Journal of Education & Development, 20*, 457–474. http://ac.els-cdn.com.ezproxy.sussex.ac.uk/S0738059300000201/1-s2.0-S0738059300000201-main.pdf?_tid=3acdcfda-7247-11e7-863a-00000aacb361&acdnat=1501103771_6eeb333a46b7152ec90543da6fff5797

Darling-Hammond, L. (1999). Teacher quality and student achievement: A review of state 278 policy evidence. Centre for the Study of Teaching and Policy, University of Washington, https://www.education.uw.edu/ctp/sites/default/files/ctpmail/PDFs/LDH_1999.pdf.

Desimone, L. M. (2009). Improving impact studies of teachers' professional development: Toward better conceptualizations and measures. *Educational Researcher, 3*(38), 181–199.

Economic Planning Unit, O. (2015). Eleventh Malaysia plan (2016–2020): Anchoring growth on people. *Percetakan Nasional Malaysia Berhad.* www.slideshare.net/mazlan1/11th-malaysia-plan-20162020

Effandi, Z., & Zanatun, I. (2007). Promoting cooperative learning in science and mathematics education: A Malaysian perspective. *Eurasia Journal of Mathematics, Science & Technology Education, 3*(1), 35–39.

Elbaz, F. (1983). *Teacher thinking. A study of practical knowledge.* Nichols Publishing.

Emaliana, I. (2017). Teacher-centered or student-centered learning approach to promote learning? *Jurnal Sosial Humaniora, 10*, 59–70. www.google.com/url?sa=t&rct=j&q=&esrc=s&source=web&cd=12&ved=2ahUKEwi02trB7KzkAhVM8HMBHUtbD5E4ChAWMAF6BAgEEAE&url=http%3A%2F%2Fiptek.its.ac.id%2Findex.php%2Fjsh%2Farticle%2Fdownload%2F2161%2F2425&usg=AOvVaw24xmdoNx1SXPXlyKtlTij7

Farrel, T. S. C., & Benisi, K. (2013). Reflecting on ESL teacher beliefs and classroom practices: A case study. *Regional Language Centre (RELC) Journal, 44*(2), 163–176. https://doi.org/10.1177/0033688213488463

Garet, M. S., Porter, A. C., Desimone, L., Birman, B. F., & Yoon, K. S. (2001). What makes professional development effective? Results from a national sample of teachers. *American Educational Research Journal, 4*(38), 915–945.

Gerard, L. F., Varma, K., Corliss, S. B., & Linn, M. C. (2011). Professional development for technology-enhanced inquiry science. *Review of Educational Research, 81*, 408–448.

Gopala, K. S. N., Roszainora, S., Nor Zaitolakma, A. S., Raja Nurul Huda, R. Z., Azyanee, L., Thenmolli, V., & Haslina, C. N,. (2014). Teachers' Knowledge and Issues in the Implementation of School-Based Assessment: A Case of Schools in Terengganu. *Asian Social Science, 10*(3), 1911–2025.

Grierson, A. L., & Woloshyn, V. E. (2013). Walking the talk: Supporting teachers' growth with differentiated professional learning. *Professional Development in Education, 39*, 401–419.

Guskey, T. R. (2002). Professional development and teacher change. *Teachers and Teaching: Theory and Practice, 8*(3/4). http://citeseerx.ist.psu.edu/viewdoc/download?doi=10.1.1.473.2693&rep=rep1&type=pdf

Hassan, R., Abdul Halim, R., & Syed Iman, S. S. J. (2006). Training Program Evaluation Institute Aminuddin Baki: A Review of the Program NPQH Cohort 9/2005. National Seminar on Management and Leadership Education.

Hazri, J., Nordin, A. R., Raju, R., & Abdul Rashid, M. (2011). *Teacher professional development in Malaysia: Issues and challenges*. Africa-Asia University Dialogue for Educational Development Report of the International Experience Sharing Seminar: Actual Status and Issues of Teacher Professional Development. CICE Series 5, 85–102.

Heller, J., Daehler, K., Wong, N., Shinohara, M., & Miratrix, L. (2012). Differential effects of three professional developments models on teacher knowledge and student achievement in elementary science. *Journal of Research in Science Teaching, 49*, 333–362.

Hussin, S. (2002). *Dasar inovasi pendidikan dalam konteks agenda wawasan 2020* [Innovation policies of education in the context of Vision 2020 agenda]. University of Malaya Press.

Jaba, S. (2013). *Availability relationships, acceptance, operation and life skills teacher concerns with integrated agricultural: Practice school based assessment*. University Putra Malaysia (UPM).

Jala, I. (2010). The crux of the matter is quality education. *Malaysian Insider*. www. themalaysianinsider.com/breakingviews/article/

Kennedy, A. (2005). Models of continuing professional development: A framework for analysis. *Journal of in-Service Education, 2*(31), 235–250.

Knapp, M. (2003). Professional development as a policy pathway. *Review of Research in Education, 27*, 109–157.

Lee, E. (2012, August 8). Why the rush to change. *The Star Online*. www.thestar.com. my/opinion/letters/2012/08/08/why-the-rush-to-change/

Loucks-Horsley, S., & Matsumoto, C. (1999). Research on professional development for teachers of mathematics and science: The state of the scene. *School Science and Mathematics, 5*(99), 258–271.

Luft, J. A., Firestone, J. B., Wong, S. S., Ortega, I., Adams, K., & Bang, E. (2011). Beginning secondary science teacher induction: A two-year mixed methods study. *Journal of Research in Science Teaching, 48*, 1199–1224.

Luft, J. A., & Hewson, P. W. (2014). *Research on teacher professional development programs in science* (N. G. Lede, Ed.). Routledge.

Macbeath, J. (2012). Future of teaching profession. *Education International*. www. educ.cam.ac.uk/centres/lfl/

Majid, F. A. (2011). School-based assessment in Malaysian schools: The concerns of English teachers. *Journal of US-China Education Review, 8*(10). http://education. uitm.edu.my/v1/images/stories/publication/faizah/article7.pdf

Malakolunthu, S., & Kwan Hoon, S. (2010). Teacher perspective of school-based assessment in a secondary school in Kuala Lumpur. *Procedia Social and Behavioural Csiences, 9*, 1170–1176. http://ac.els-cdn.com/S1877042810024079/1-s2.0-S1877042810024079-main.pdf?_tid=1f4cb79a-6ef9-11e7-ae85-00000aab0f26&acdnat=1500740371_a280189292236d3aa82c3b115fed21d7

Mat Yusoff, M. A., Ahmad, J., Mansor, A. N., Johari, R., Othman, K., & Che Hassan, N. (2016). Evaluation of school based assessment teacher training programme. *Scientific Research Publishing, 7*, 627–638. http://file.scirp.org/pdf/CE_2016042014464663.pdf

McRobbie, C. J., & Tobin, K. (1995). Restraints to reform: The congruence of teacher and student actions in a chemistry classroom. *Journal of Research in Science Education, 4*(32), 373–385.

Messick, S. (1994). The interplay of evidence and consequences in the validation of performance assessment. *Educational Researcher, 23*(3), 13–23.

MoE Malaysia. (2013). *Malaysia education blueprint 2013–2025* (Preschool to Post-Secondary Education).

MoE Malaysia. (2015). *Malaysia education blueprint 2015–2025 (Higher Education) (p. A-1)*. Kementerian Pendidikan Malaysia. www.mohe.gov.my/en/download/public/penerbitan/pppm-2015-2025-pt/5-malaysia-education-blueprint-2015-2025-higher-education/file

Mohd Asari, S. (2013). *School based assessment for UPSR: An evaluation towards a national assessment system transformation*. University Kebangsaan Malaysia (UKM).

Moidunny, K. (2009). *National principalship qualification effectiveness program (NPQH)*. University Kebangsaan Malaysia (UKM).

Ng, L. Y., Kamariah, A. B., Samsilah, R., Wong, S. L., & Petri Zabariah, M. A. R. (2005). Predictors of self-regulated learning in Malaysian smart schools. *International Education Journal, 6*(3), 343–353.

OECD. (2009). Creating effective teaching and learning environments: First results from TALIS. In *OECD Publishing*. OECD Publications. https://doi.org/10.1787/9789264068780-en

Osman, A. M., & Kassim, A. R. (2013). *Transforming the teaching profession in Malaysia*. Genting Highlands, Malaysia: Institute Aminudin Baki.

Ottoson, J. M. (1997). After the applause: Exploring multiple influences on application following an adult education program. *Adult Education Quarterly, 2*(47), 92–107.

Performance Management and Delivery Unit, 0. (2010). *Transforming education as an engine of growth*. http://etp.pemandu.gov.my/

Petras, Y., Jamil, H., & Mohamed, A. R. (2012). How do teachers learn? A study on the policy and practice of teacher professional development in Malaysia. *KEDI Journal of Educational Policy, 9*(1), 51–70.

Phoi Ching, C., & Peng Yee, C. (2012). Primary teacher education in Malaysia. *International Education Research, 8*(4). www.cluteinstitute.com/ojs/index.php/JIER/article/view/7285/7353

Pianta, R. C. (2011). Teaching children well: New evidence based approaches to teacher professional development and training. *Center for American Progress, 11*, 1–36.

Porter, A. C., Garet, M., Desimone, L., Yoon, K. S., & Birman, B. (2000). *Does professional development change teachers' instruction? Results from a three-year study of the effects of Eisenhower and other professional development on teaching practice*. The American Institutes for Research, Washington, D.C., https://files.eric.ed.gov/fulltext/ED455227.pdf.

Resnick, L. B., & Resnick, D. P. (1991). Assessing the thinking curriculum: New tools for educational reform. In B. R. Giggord & M. C. O'Çonner (Eds.), *Changing assessments: Alternative views of aptitude, achievement and instruction* (pp. 37–75). Kluwer.

Richard, J. C., & Rodgers, T. (2001). *Approaches and methods in language teaching*. Cambridge University Press.

Robertson, S. L. (2005). Re-imagining and rescripting the future of education global knowledge economy discourses and the challenge to education systems. *Comparative Education, 41*(2), 151–170.

SEAMEO INNOTECH. (2010). Teaching Competency Standards in Southeast Asian Countries: Eleven Country Audit. Southeast Asian Ministers of Education Organisation, *Regional Centre for Educational Innovation and Technology*.

Shanusi, A. (2007). *An investigation of teachers' readiness towards school based assessment scheme in selected Malaysian teacher training institutes.* www.iaea.info/documents/paper_1162b276b3.pdf

Siti Suriani, O. (2007, May 31). Piawaian bertaraf dunia angkat imej Guru. *Berita Harian, 10.* http://ddms.usim.edu.my/bitstream/123456789/1957/1/31Mei 2007-SURAT%26 E-MEL%2810%29.pdf

Smith, T., & Ingersoll, R. (2004). What are the effects of induction and mentoring on beginning teacher turnover? *American Educational Research Journal, 41,* 681–714.

Sobri, A. A. (2011, September 21). Guru merungut program SAPS lebih sukar dari manual. *Berita Harian.*

Spillane, J. P. (2002). The pedagogy of district policies and programs. *Teachers College Record, 104,* 377–420.

Stillman, G. (2001). The impact of school-based assessment on the implementation of a modelling/applications-based curriculum: An Australia example. *Teaching Mathematics and Its Application, 20*(3), 101–107.

Swee Choo Goh, P. (2012). The Malaysian teacher standards: A look at the challenges and implications for teachers educators. *Educational Research Policy and Practice, 11,* 73–87. https://eric.ed.gov/?id=EJ967221

Talib, R., Abu Naim, H., & Mat Hassan, M. A. (2014). *School-based assessment: A study on teacher's knowledge and practices.* International Graduate Conference on Engineering, Science and Humanities (IGCESH). www.researchgate.net/publication/277562401_SCHOOL-BASED_ASSESSMENT_A_STUDY_ON_TEACHER%27S_KNOWLEDGE_AND_PRACTICES

Tobin, K., & Lamaster, S. (1995). Relationship between metaphors, beliefs and actions in a context of science curriculum change. *Journal of Science, 32*(3), 225–242.

Torrance, H. (1995). *Evaluating authentic assessment: Problems and possibilities in new approaches to assessment.* Open University Press.

UNESCO. (2015). *Education for all 2015 national review report: Malaysia.* http://unesdoc.unesco.org/images/0022/002297/229719E.pdf

UNESCO. (2017). Education for sustainable development goals. *Learning Objectives,* p. 67. *United Nations Educational, Scientific and Cultural Organisation,* https://unesdoc.unesco.org/ark:/48223/pf0000247444.

Vethamani, M. E. (2011). Teacher education in Malaysia: Preparing and training of English language teacher education. *The Journal of Asia Tefl, 8*(4), 85–110.

Wallin, J. (2003). Improving school effectiveness, Vancouver. *ABAC Journal, 23*(1), 61–72.

Wei, R. C., Darling-Hammond, L., and Adamson, F. (2010). Professional development in the United States: Trends and challenges. Dallas, TX. National Staff Development Council.

Westbrook, J. (2017). *Assessing teachers: Quality and accountability.* Lecture note, Teachers: Policy and Practice in International Context, 810X3, University of Sussex, delivered 27 February 2017.

Yap, K. C. (2004). *Teaching primary science.* Pearson/Prentice Hall.

Yew Tee, M., Samuel, M., Mohd Nor, N. bin, & Hutkemri, R. A. V. S. (2018). Classroom practice and the quality of teaching: Where a nation is going? *Journal of International and Comparative Education, 7*(1), 17–33. https://doi.org/10.14425/jice.2018.7.1.17

Zakaria, A. (2000). Educational Development and Reformation in the Malaysian Education System: Challenges in the New Millennium. *Journal of Southeast Asian Education, 1*(1), 113–133. www.academia.edu/8549539/Educational_Development_and_Reformation_in_the_Malaysian_Education_System_Challenges_in_the_New_Millennium?auto=download

Zamri, S. N. A. S. (2016). Problem-solving skills among Malaysian students. In L. M. Thien (Ed.), *What can PISA 2012 data tell us?* SensePublishers. https://doi.org/10.1007/978-94-6300-468-8_7

Zeichner, K., & Ndimande, B. (2008). Contradictions and tensions in the place of teachers in educational reform: Reflections on teacher preparation in the USA and Namibia. *Teachers and Teaching: Theory and Practice, 14*(4), 331–343. https://doi.org/10.1080/13540600802037751

6 Experiencing Blended Language Learning in Malaysia Public Higher Education Institution

Shukor, Siti Shuhaida

Introduction

English has been taught to Malaysians since the 1960s (Omar, 1992) as one of the compulsory subjects in the national curriculum during primary education (six to 12 years old), secondary school (13–17 years old) as well as post-secondary and tertiary levels of education (18 years and above). I was five years old when I was introduced to the English language. When I was at university, English became a compulsory requirement (Malaysian Examination Councils, 2006). As a Malaysian adult, I have learned English for 14 to 15 years. I believe this is average for Malaysians who started learning English from the tender age of 5/6. However, the long exposure to learning English does not guarantee language competency. Fewer than 50% of students who completed primary education at 12 years old achieved the national standard of English language (EPU, 2016, p. 10). The same is evident in the higher education system where Malaysian graduates can experience difficulty finding employment due to low level proficiency in English language (Singh & Singh, 2008). Melor and Rashidah's (2011) study also reported falling levels of English language proficiency among Malaysians, including those in tertiary education. Low levels of English Proficiency are seen as a threat to the country's aspirations of being a fully developed and economically competitive nation.

In addressing English language proficiency problems, I remember the Ministry of Education and the Government of Malaysia produced strategic reinforcement plans for education with the common goal of enhancing the quality of English language proficiency throughout the nation. One of the proposed elements was to include technology. From the higher education perspective, many institutions have sought to integrate ICT (Information and Communications Technology) into their teaching (Lee et al., 2008) and also outside classroom learning. This is where Blended Learning (BL) comes into the picture. BL describes a combination of learning environments, typically classroom or face-to-face (f2f) teaching and distance or online learning. In BL, it is common for students to be asked to study at home and bring their experiences to

DOI: 10.4324/9781003374190-6

the classroom. However, as someone who has experienced BL, I believe the core principles of BL revolve around collaborative learning, student-centred, and more inclusive practices and processes. BL also has the capacity to give students more control over their learning in terms of when, where and how, to do it, as well as the pace of learning within a more personalised environment (Staker & Horn, 2012).

The purpose of BL, in my understanding, is to enrich the quality of instruction in the face to face (f2f) classroom by enriching it with online learning elements for the benefit of both students and teachers. I believe that BL can improve teaching conditions for teachers. From the students' perspective, BL offers an opportunity to experience a more personalised and technically enriched learning environment. For these reasons, BL has attracted noticeable interest and support (Mohamed Amin Embi, 2011); as well as promoted by the government, systems such as Moodle, eLMS, MOOCS – to name a few – have been introduced as vehicles for online teaching and learning Most tertiary education institutions acknowledge the merits of using BL as meeting the diverse needs of students as well as assisting the teaching and learning process (Mohamed Amin Embi, 2011; Ling et al., 2010). Researchers in Malaysia have also found that BL increases accessibility to learning materials, reduces the class time needed, allows more interesting lessons, creates a student-centred learning environment, and offers flexible time and location for learning (Haron et al., 2012; Lim, 2010; Siew-Eng & Muuk, 2015; Siew et al., 2012; Thang et al., 2013; Wai & Seng, 2013).

Due to its perceived advantages and benefits, BL models have been included in the Malaysian Education Blueprint, Wave 1 (2013–2015). However, the National Education Blueprint ideal seems far away from reality. Malaysia, unfortunately, is still one step behind in comparison to other developed countries when it comes to implementing BL (Maznah, 2004). Thus, I believe it is significant to ask why BL has not taken off well. Are there any challenges to its implementation? Is there anything missing? These questions keep playing back and forth of my head and I feel the urge to find the answers.

In helping me to find answers, I gathered research articles and journals on BL from a language perspective. I found that many research studies on the subject of BL have used different theoretical models to explain BL teaching and learning from a language learning perspective. However, I found very little work focusing on the opportunities and obstacles of incorporating ICT in a holistic manner, or theories providing a more rounded framework to explore learning changes. From further exploration, I identified cultural-historical activity theory (CHAT) as offering a way of looking at innovation more holistically. Therefore, in this chapter, I would like to reflect on the BL take up through the five elements of CHAT.

Cultural-Historical Activity Theory (CHAT)

Due to the part of political climate during the Cold War and its adherence to Marxist ideals, cultural-historical activity theory was initially restricted to the Soviet Union. Many years later, Engestrom (1987) has made CHAT more popular dan accepted at a wider range underpinning of Activity Theory (AT). 'Activity' that makes up the smallest unit, is considered as the most fundamental element in this theory. AT has always emphasised the collective character of human daily activity whereby the collective aspect is concretely achieved by an individual at a particular cultural-historical period and location. AT analyses the process of human activity and human thought within a specific context through a historical and socio-cultural lens (Engeström, 1999; Jonassen & Rohrer-Murphy, 1999). However, the development of AT with the cultural and historical element making up CHAT offers a more holistic framework to investigate the relationships between the elements present within a particular system or context. Besides a methodological framework, CHAT also offers practical tools to apply in various contexts, including education. Research studies in education have used the AT framework for analysing different aspects of teaching and learning including ICT (e.g. Blin & Appel, 2011; Gedera, 2014; Timmis, 2014).

There have been three generations of CHAT. Figure 6.1 shows the first generation revolved around three key principles: human subjects use tools to achieve an object. Vygotsky argued that human relationships with objects are not straightforward. Society and culture are two elements that influence that relationship, while psychological tools such as language and thinking control physical activity These cultural-historical psychology tools emerge from human activity mediated by artifacts (tools) and signs.

Figure 6.1 shows that in an activity system, it is motivated by the object and in achieving the object, it is mediated by one or more artifacts which is also called as tools. Subject employs the tools towards the object resulting to

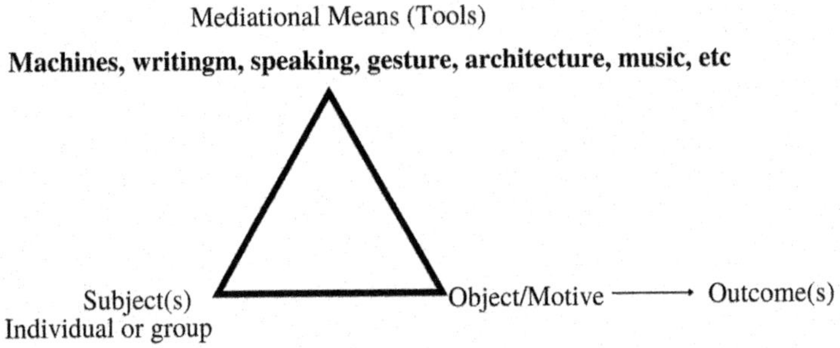

Mediational Means (Tools)

Machines, writingm, speaking, gesture, architecture, music, etc

Subject(s)
Individual or group

Object/Motive ⟶ Outcome(s)

Figure 6.1 First generation of activity theory

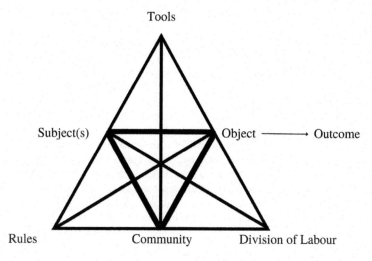

Figure 6.2 Second generation of activity theory

either desired or undesired outcome. Having a conscious motive often results to goal-directed actions where dialectical relation is imposed.

The second generation of CHAT developed by Leontiev (1974) visualises six different elements making up: actors (subjects), objects (goals/motivation), mediation tools, division of labour, community as well as rules (see Figure 6.2). The system is depicted as a series of triangles within an all-encompassing outer triangle to show the inter-relationships between all the elements. Activities are seen as a collective at the core of which a subject is striving to achieve an object or goal. Leontiev (1974) further describes the object-oriented activity as:

'a unit of life mediated by mental reflection whose real function is to orient the subject to the world of objects. Activity is thus not a reaction or a totality of reactions, but rather a system possessing structure, inner transformations, conversations, and development'

(p. 10)

For Leontiev (1974), CHAT analyses human interaction as occurring within a group of processes. At the core of activity theory is the idea of a subject, that is, a person trying to achieve a goal/object. However, this always takes place in a context which shapes the activity of the subject. This context is influenced by the rules, community, and division of labour. For Leontiev, activity is driven by how an individual make sense of their environment, which depends on the physical and cultural characteristic of the environment.

In activity theory, each element is in a relationship with all the others. For instance, the subject's action is influenced by the object, while the object is influenced by how the subject uses the available tools to mediate the teaching/learning process. Activity is a reciprocal process involving the subject, the object and the relationship between the two and their context (Davydov, 1999). Cultural activities and structures are formulated within an activity (Engeström & Miettinen, 1999; Leontiev, 1974).

Engeström further developed the third generation of CHAT, the relationship between the individual, artefacts and behaviour (Engeström et al., 1999) (see Figure 6.3). Engeström acknowledges the dynamic nature of the activity system; the system is not static but can or has to adapt to changes. For instance, when new mediation tools are introduced, the existing tools can be a hindrance to the implementation of the new ones. Hence, tensions/contradictions might interrupt the smooth process of system. His key point is that an activity system comes with contradictions, and understanding those contradictions enables people to identify what is holding up change and to work out what to do about it (Blin & Munro, 2008; Timmis, 2014).

Figure 6.3 presents the overlapping between two sets of activities/processes occurring at the same time, so each process as a set of actions, can affect the other. Engeström's (1999) representation of third generation Activity Theory takes account of two interacting activities. According to Engeström (1987), actions are usually intentional and carried out through a series of routinised and automated operations which are mediated by artefacts/tools either materials (books, computers, machinery) or psychological (language, sign systems, models). This third CHAT generation makes the importance of the community element (participants who take part in the same activity) clearer, and the rules and division of labour (to show how work is organised). Contradictions in the activity system may trigger innovation and can be a source of development (Barab et al., 2002; Blin & Munro, 2008; Engeström, 1987, 2001; Helle, 2000). Engeström (1999) saw the subject as not the only main agent of change, but also the environment should be considered as a part of the factor that causes changes within and between activity systems. New activity systems occur with the 'reflective appropriation of advanced models

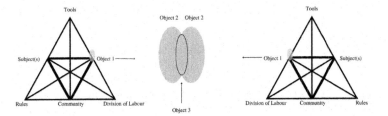

Figure 6.3 Third generation of activity theory

Table 6.1 Summary of CHAT elements

Element	Description
Tools (Artifact)	• An artifact is an aspect of the material world that has been modified over the history of its incorporation into goal-directed human action (Cole, 1996)
Subject (Agency)	• The relation between subject and object: asymmetrical • Ability to produce effects • The agent is the subject of activity with the ability and means to act • The real-life study of technology: a part of unfolding human interaction with the world in general
Object	• What action is directed towards • Motivates activities • Separates one activity from another • Dynamic: transforms as the activity unfolds • Available tools and signs
Rules	• Explicit and implicit • Norms and values • Conventions and standards constraining action
Division of labour	• Participation in socially distributed work activities • Individual action: motivation by one object but directed towards another
Community	• Individuals/social groups who share the same general object

and tools' as 'ways out of internal contradictions' (Cole & Engeström, 1993, p. 40). CHAT has been used to look at technologically integrated activities based on the view that what people think, and feel is entangled with what people do (see Daniels et al., 2010; Kaptelinin & Nardi, 2006; Roth & Lee, 2007). CHAT elements can thus be useful to capture more holistically the relationships between users, technology and the outcome for educational technology integration and BL take up. Table 6.1 shows a summary of these elements.

The Use of BL in English Language Teaching Context

To support the government's aspirations, the shift in teaching became apparent when all instructors are required or expected to integrate the use of learning management system (LMS) into their teaching. This involved attending many training sessions to improve computer literacy skills, especially concerning the learning management platform. Having gone through several trainings and had first-hand experience conducting blended learning in my courses made me aware of the difficulties educators face in transferring skills and communicating via the use of technology. Even technology enthusiasts passionate to improve their teaching pedagogy with technology can face challenges and obstacles in their teaching, so others with less interest in technology can have

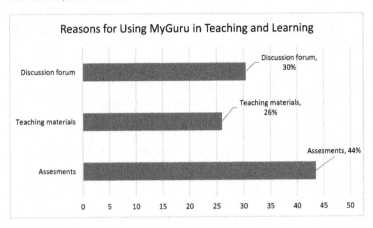

Figure 6.4 Reasons for using BL in teaching

even more concerns. For this reason, I took the next step to find the views of other educators.

I carried out a survey to 16 language teachers from the same the institution to help identify their motives for implementing blended learning as well as the challenges they had along the process. The responses were then categorised and analysed. Many of the language teachers were mostly interested in using BL for assessment purposes such as self-access quizzes and tests including submitting assignments (see Figure 6.4). These activities involved the use of Google Form, Survey Monkey, MyGuru (an LMS platform provided by the institution to all its academic staff), and the most basic form of online communication, emails. Apart from that, the majority of language teachers used BL for online discussion forums like MyGuru and Google Classroom since this platform is ready made on MyGuru for instance, and for distributing teaching material in note form (Word, PDF, PPT) as well as video sharing via links not only in MyGuru, but other available online platforms such as YouTube, Google Drive, and Google Classroom.

From my own preference, I blended my teaching with technology to make it more appealing, especially by integrating the five multimedia elements – text, images, audio, animation and video – in the belief that students pay more attention during blended lessons, so helping them to comprehend the subject matter better. I always believe this is one of the advantages of incorporating technology into the delivery of education the education fraternity should be aware of. However, the survey revealed the majority of respondents still preferred to teach in a f2f setting rather than online with an average of 67.2% of responses for all language learning skills including grammar. Further breakdown shows the most striking preference using face-to-face teaching in grammar with 71% and speaking skills with 89% during the brick-and-mortar classroom sessions. Perhaps this preference is due to the advantage of getting immediate feedback and direct physical interaction which is more appropriate for a language learning classroom. Teaching grammar puts emphasis on the conventions of the system and structure of a language whilst speaking focuses on the ability to communicate effectively in the target language. Both can be done effectively in a f2f setting and more visible responses and participations on the usage can be observed directly in a physical classroom setting.

When teachers used online teaching, I notice more focus was given to listening skills, perhaps due to the resources that are widely available online. For instance, listening to native speakers converse on an online platform provides learners with an authentic experience and they can replay the audio as many times as they want. Teaching listening skills was the preferred skill in a blended learning environment.

These findings triggered further exploration. This was when I referred to five CHAT elements; I created a number of statements representing teachers views on their readiness and achievements in using BL in English language teaching context.

Subject

The following statements refer to teachers' readiness to use BL in their teaching, which teacher respondents could either agree or disagree with. There were five spectrums for the responses ranging from strongly disagree, somewhat disagree, neither agree nor disagree, somewhat agree as well as strongly agree. For example, '*I felt pedagogically prepared to teach this course*', '*I felt technically prepared to teach this course*', and '*My teaching style matches well with BL*'. From the items, the majority of teachers agreed that they felt pedagogically (14 teachers) and technically prepared (13 teachers) to teach their course taking a BL approach. They also agreed that that teaching using BL matched their teaching style with 11 responses. Thus, this implies that the teachers might have had a good degree of readiness to take on the use of MyGuru and classroom instruction. From the CHAT perspective, the language teachers had positive attitudes, suggesting they went beyond their basic role as teachers, that is, to teach solely and regarded each individual learner as unique – which BL fosters.

Rules

With regard to rules, three statements were created for teachers to respond to, two aimed to discover if teachers were aware of the institution regulations where they worked: '*I followed the course organisation as stated in the course guidelines*'; and '*I followed the guidelines provided by the university when implementing BL*'. Another statement aimed to find out if the teachers 'explained the course rules and regulations to students at the beginning of the course'. The responses showed that all the teachers claimed to have explained the course rules and regulations to the students when the course started and followed the course organisation and guidelines set by the university. This suggests the teachers had a high degree of compliance with the university expectations. From the CHAT perspective, the university had set the rules prior to the blended learning courses and all language teachers indicated their awareness of the rules although the rules might not have been articulated orally. Ten language teachers had responded to somewhat agree whilst another five had chosen strongly to agree where they claimed they followed the designated rules in their blended learning classes.

Division of Labour

The division of labour revolves around teacher/student participation and activities in the BL context. They agreed or disagreed with a set of statements that were given to them as follows: '*I encouraged students to participate in BL activities*', '*I discussed with my colleagues regarding teaching material*', '*I consulted with my course coordinator regarding activities on MyGuru and in the classroom*', '*Managing the classroom activities was easy*', '*I made an effort to integrate classroom and online activities with each other*', '*I worked together with other colleagues when designing the course activities*', '*I acted as a facilitator in MyGuru*', '*I did not interact with students in MyGuru and only monitored them from afar*', and '*Managing the online activities was easy*'. From the responses, 16 teachers indicated they had encouraged students to participate in BL. Thirteen had also discussed teaching materials and course activities with their colleagues and course coordinator. Thirteen rated their experience in managing the class as easy. Therefore, 14 had made efforts to combine f2f and online activities. Discussions with colleagues about designing activities had been useful.

Teachers' role became that of a facilitator they only monitored students' engagement from afar without any interaction with them online. However, teachers were uncertain on how to rate their experience of managing online activities. However, their responses suggest a balance in terms of task distribution between teachers and colleagues. From the CHAT perspective, the division of labour had both a vertical and horizontal hierarchy structure. The vertical organisational structure showed power emanating from top to bottom when teachers sought advice from course coordinators, while the horizontal structure shows no hierarchy; the teachers shared the tasks without a middle management team.

Community

The statements in relation to community aimed to see whether teachers gained the support they needed to implement BL. The statements include '*The university monitored the activities in my BL course*', '*I received the BL pedagogical support I needed during the course*', '*I received the technical support I needed during this course*', '*I received feedback on how to conduct my teaching*', '*The university has provided training for the BL implementation*', '*Getting technical support was easy*', and '*I attended the BL training sessions*'. Based on their responses, 12 teachers agreed the university had monitored their engagement in BL and that they had received pedagogical and technical support throughout the course. However, eight teachers were undecided whether they received feedback on their teaching conduct, three teachers were uncertain whether the university had provided training to use BL nor had attended any training sessions (two teachers). Concerning technical support, teachers found this procedure as neither easy nor difficult, but seven teachers said they had received the necessary support for BL implementation despite some uncertainties. Community from the CHAT perspective refers to how the university, at the meso level, contributed to the blended learning activity system by providing training and support.

Outcomes

Based on CHAT, outcomes are the object or a goal a subject aims to achieve. It involves what action is directed towards this goal and the transformation that takes place as the activity unfolds. Statements to help teachers reflect were developed on what they found successful or unsuccessful in using BL for them to respond to. '*I had enough influence on the course contents and activities*', '*I would like to teach other ESL courses using BL*', '*The classroom activities were successfully executed*', '*I managed to meet the learning objectives at the end of the course*', '*The MyGuru activities were successfully executed*', '*Students were more active during the classroom activities*', '*The classroom activities worked well*', '*I found students had actively participated during MyGuru activities*', '*I prefer classroom activities more than MyGuru activities*', '*There was a good balance between online and classroom activities*', '*The online and classroom activities integrated well*', '*The online activities worked well*', '*Integrating the online and classroom activities was easy*' either , '*Students were more active during the MyGuru activities*', '*I did not face any difficulties while teaching in MyGuru*', and '*Using BL did not make this course more demanding to teach*'.

From the responses to the statements above, 14 teachers agreed they had enough influence on the course contents and activities, so they liked teaching other ESL courses in the BL mode. Fifteen teachers agreed that they managed to successfully execute f2f activities slightly better than the online activities.

This, according to them, contributed to the achievement of their learning goals at the end of the course. Eleven teachers agreed that their students were active in their physical lesson but slightly more active in online activities (12 teachers), suggesting online activities worked better than physical classroom. Even though teachers wanted to use BL more, they still preferred to have more classroom activities than online, probably because students psychomotor and cognitive domains could be visibly observed than in the online classroom where limited vision of these domains might be clouded as there was no access via the online platform. This however, does not mean the online activities did not work well – 11 teachers found a combination of online and classroom activities integrated well. Both medium works well but in terms of preferences, teachers still prefer to have physical classroom setting. Nonetheless, seven teachers rated their experiences of integrating f2f and online modes as neither easy nor difficult. There were mixed views about whether their students were more active in MyGuru activities than in the physical classroom and or whether teaching using BL was demanding or not, which implies that BL teaching might be quite challenging for some. What made it interesting about blended learning is that, from the outcome's perspective, face-to-face mode was still perceived as preferable to online teaching. Fifteen teachers also implied that they successfully conducted f2f teaching better than online teaching. This suggests blended learning, in particular, online work might cause difficulties for some teachers for many underlying reasons. Although 11 teachers acknowledged the incorporation of face-to-face and online teaching enhanced their students' learning experience, they were uncertain of students' engagement during the class most probably because lack of observable behaviour online during the lesson which the online platform does not have access to it.

Sixteen teachers who completed the pre- and post-surveys were pedagogically and technically ready to venture into BL teaching, reflected in their use of online settings for online assessment, discussion forums as well as teaching material sharing. They also showed compliance to the university and students' expectation based on the responses from the survey. Their role during the online session was only as facilitator via remote monitoring rather than being actively involved in interactions. In terms of support, the teachers agreed that their university had played a role in monitoring their BL teaching. This could be due to the organising of a series of townhall, guidelines and manual book to help the teachers in using the online platform. Nonetheless, 7 out of 16 teachers were uncertain about the feedback on their BL teaching and training received on the use of BL. Nine teachers also rated the technical support received as neither easy nor difficult to get, probably because they did not even ask for it as they were comfortable with BL. This could explain why the outcomes from BL implementation were rather positive even though 14 teachers might feel that BL was demanding to do in addition to obstacles faced during their teaching.

What Have I learned?

The results of the study suggest technology has changed the way people communicate. Digital devices and technology have created opportunities for bridging physical distance in respect to social contact and with global and local impact on economic, socio-cultural and political structures (Papacharissi, 2010). For example, digital archives allow wider access to archive material, while interactive multimedia allows for more engaging participation, and expanded social networks allow ubiquitous reach. The proliferation of ICT in education has sparked considerable interest among scholars as well as institution leaders and stakeholders. For some people, technology has made communication more superficial, thus threatening relationships. However, digital media can be a flexible, powerful tool offering benefits from establishing stronger bonds and connections. Offline and online spheres of social contact, for instance, are facilitated by multimedia platforms in ways that have positive effects on social capital (Bauernschuster et al., 2011; Ellison et al., 2007; Hampton & Wellman, 2003; Papacharissi, 2010).

Technology can appeal to young people in positive ways (Prensky, 2001); enhancing support for content area learning (Kinzer & Leu, 1997); improving reading comprehension; increasing language acquisition (Zhao, 2005); enhancing test scores (Abdul Rahman, 2018; Boster & Staff, 2004; Rajaretnam, 2004); boosting motivation (Granito & Chernobilsky, 2012); as well as self-esteem in the context of exposure to Facebook (Gonzales & Hancock, 2011). In terms of BL in language teaching and learning, technology allows students to have control over their learning regarding time, place, path as well as the pace of learning within a more personalised and conducive learning environment (Staker & Horn, 2012). More pragmatically, technology may support conventional teaching methods by providing more interactive opportunities such as interactive whiteboards, PowerPoint lecture notes and other interactive learning software.

On the other hand, technology can be forced upon education and can disrupt teaching unnecessarily, resulting in learning erosion (Coates et al., 2005; Hirschheim, 2005; Noble, 1998). In practice, the process of transforming education using technologies relies on the replication and reinforcement of teacher-led and didactic practices (Blin & Munro, 2008; Eynon, 2008; Kirkwood, 2014). ICT is assumed to be fit for replication, but in practice, local difficulties mediate its use. Selwyn (2011) claims that education technology often suffers from a top-down managerial discourse dominated by efficiency. He further asserts that 'technical fixes will only deal with the surface manifestations of a problem and not its roots' (p. 33) and that teaching and learning need to be tackled from a social issue perspective, not a technical one. He concludes that there are many claims about ICT based on suppositions, personal beliefs, opinions and conjecture. Even though technology is seen as enhancing learning, there is very little evidence of this. More conclusive evidence is needed, and this study offers suggestions using CHAT as an evaluation system, to help fill this gap.

The role of technology in language learning has never been straightforward. Many language practitioners still struggle to fully incorporate technology, particularly computer-based technology, into their teaching practice, professional development, institutional leadership and curriculum design (Motteram, 2013). The reasons for partial takeup can be insufficient pedagogical and technological knowledge – including orientation, mentorship and established policies (Ali et al., 2004) as well as lack of practical experience in planning and implementing the use of new technology. In Malaysia, the Ministry of Education identified one of the factors that contributed to the low uptake of technology-based learning as poor interface design (Kamariah, 2006; Kamaruddin, 2010; MDC, 2005). On top of that, there can be technical problems with hardware and software. The time factor, limited computer literacy; lack of instructional design resulted in irrelevant content; technical malfunctions; inefficient ICT infrastructure and insufficient hardware were all factors that led educators to avoid using the technology in their teaching (Azizah et al., 2005; Mirzajani et al., 2016; Selvaraj, 2010). Similar challenges were portrayed by the teachers who implemented BL in this study, based on the responses given in the previous subheadings. What encouraged or discouraged teachers in this study came under three key headings: access; teachers and institutions.

With regard to access, the main concern was students' ability to use the technology, for example, computer or laptop and also and access the internet. Access could be one of the most important factors in the development of educational technology. In this sense, it is a causal factor, for without technology there is no BL. Even when there is technology, teachers need the basic infrastructure such as the computer, LCD projectors, internet connection to be available and fully working in their classrooms. In addition, the software should be user-friendly, and supported by specialist staff (Firmin & Genesi, 2013). Teachers need to be able to rely on the technology and properly plan what they want to do in their lessons. With reliable technology, the amount of time and effort spent in using the VLE (virtual learning environment) can be reduced (Becta, 2004). Unreliability of technology and doubts about its performance, for instance, audio recording that cannot be heard during teaching in the classroom can discourage teachers from using technology. Teachers, on the other hand, need to be well-versed in using technology, the basic procedure to operate technology as without this, classes will not run smoothly. Interruptions during lessons can be a major drawback for both teachers and students to cope with. Computer literacy should not be a hurdle and must be established at all costs. Institutions need to play their role too by providing training and the infrastructure to support blended learning courses could help smoothen the process.

Conclusion

The implementation of blended learning requires a deeper understanding of its place and implications within education theory or at least this is what I think its supporters proposed. The blending of technology in language learning specifically can be complex because it requires both external and internal drivers (Oxford & Jung, 2007) including technology accessibility, course structure delivery, teacher acceptance and readiness, to name a few. The successful integration of this technology demands commitment in time, developing the competence to develop appropriate designs, and teaching experience as well as reflection on teaching (Moser, 2007).

References

Abdul Rahman, A. M. (2018). English writing performance using blended learning in TVET education. *Language Literacy, 2*(1), 28–36.

Ali, N., Hodson-Carlton, K., & Ryan, M. (2004). Students' perceptions of online learning: Implications for teaching. *Nurse Educator, 29*(3), 111–115.

Azizah, Y., Nor Fariza, M. N., & Hazita, A. (2005). Teaching English the SMART way. *The International Journal of English Language Learning and Teaching (IJELLT), 2*(2), 11–22.

Barab, S., Barnett, M. & Squire, K., (2002). Developing an empirical account of a community of practice: Characterizing the essential tensions. *The journal of the learning sciences, 11*(4), 489–542.

Bauernschuster, S., Falck, O., & Woessmann, L. (2011). Surfing alone? The internet and social capital: Evidence from an unforeseeable technological mistake. *Journal of Public Economics, 117*, 73–89.

Becta. (2004). *What the research says about ICT and reducing teachers' workloads.* Becta.

Blin, F., & Munro, M. (2008). Why hasn't technology disrupted academics' teaching practices? Understanding resistance to change through the lens of activity theory. *Computers & Education, 50*(2), 475–490.

Blin, F. & Appel, C., (2011). Computer supported collaborative writing in practice: An activity theoretical study. *CALICO Journal, 28*(2), 473–497.

Boster, F. J., & Staff. (2004). *2004 United streaming evaluation: 6th and 8th grade mathematics in the Los Angeles unified school district.* Cometrika, Inc.

Coates, H., James, R., & Baldwin, G. (2005). A critical examination of the effects of learning management systems on university teaching and learning. *Tertiary Education and Management, 11*(1), 19–36.

Cole, M. (1996). *Cultural psychology: A once and future discipline.* The Belknap Press of Harvard University Press.

Cole, M. & Engeström, Y., (1993). A cultural-historical approach to distributed cognition, In G Saloman (Ed.), *Distributed cognitions: Psychological and educational considerations,* New York: Cambridge University Press.

Daniels, H., Edwards, A., Engestrom, Y., Gallagher, Tony, Ludvigsen, S. (2010). *Activity Theory in Practice. Promoting learning across boundaries and agencies.* Routledge London.

Davydov, Vassily V. (1999). The content and unsolved problems of activity theory. In Yrjö Engeström, Reijo Miettinen & Raija-Leena Punamäki-Gitai (eds.), *Perspectives on Activity Theory*. Cambridge University Press. 39–52.

Ellison, N. B., Steinfeld, C., & Lampe, C. (2007). TOIL: The benefits of Facebook "friends:" Social capital and college students use of online social network sites. *Journal of Computer-Mediated Communication, 12*(4), 1143–1168.

Engeström, Y., (1987). *Learning by expanding: an activity-theoretical approach to development research*, Helsinki, Finland: Orienta-Konsultit.

Engeström, Y., (1999). 23 Innovative learning in work teams: Analyzing cycles of knowledge creation in practice. In Y., Engeström, E., Miettinen & R.L., Punamaki-Gitai (Eds). *Perspectives on activity theory*. Cambridge: Cambridge University Press, 377–404.

Engeström, Y., Miettinen, R., & Punamäki, R.-L. (Eds.). (1999). Perspectives on activity theory. Cambridge University Press. pp. 377-404. https://doi.org/10.1017/CBO9780511812774

EPU. (2016). *Transforming education system*, Chapter 6th Strategy paper 10: Eleventh Economic Malaysian Plan, Economic Planning Unit: Putrajaya.

Eynon, R. (2008). The use of the world wide web in learning and teaching in higher education: Reality and rhetoric. *Innovations in Education & Teaching International, 45*(1), 15–23.

Firmin, M. W., & Genesi, D. J. (2013). History and implementation of classroom technology. *Procedia Social and Behavioural Sciences, 93*(2013), 1603–1617.

Gedera, D.S.P., (2014). Tool mediation and learner engagement : An activity theory perspective. In B. Hegrty, J. McDonald., & S, -K. Loke (Eds),. In *Rhetoric and Reality: Critical Perspectives on Educational Conference Proceedings*. Dunedin, New Zeland, 42–48.

Gonzales, A. L., & Hancock, J. T. (2011). Mirror, mirror on my Facebook wall: Effects of exposure to Facebook on self-esteem. *Cyberpsychology, Behavior, and Social Networking, 14*(1–2), 79–83.

Granito, M., & Chernobilsky, E. (2012). The effect of technology on a student's motivation and knowledge retention. In *NERA conference proceedings 2012*. University of Connecticut, 19 October, 1–22.

Hampton, K., & Wellman, B. (2003). Neighboring in Netville: How the internet supports community and social capital in a wired suburb? *City & Community, 2*(4), 277–311.

Haron, H., Abbas, W. F., & Rahman, N. A. A. (2012). The adoption of blended learning among Malaysian academicians. *Procedia – Social and Behavioral Sciences, 67*, 175–181.

Helle, M., (2000). Disturbances and contradictions as tools for understanding work in the newsroom. *Scandinavian Journal of Information Systems*, 12, 81–114.

Hirschheim, R. (2005). The Internet-based education bandwagon: Look before you leap. *Communications of the ACM, 48*(7), 97–101.

Jonassen, D.H. & Rohrer-Murphy, L., (1999). Activity theory as a framework for designing constructivist learning environments. *Educational Technology Research and Development, 47*(1), 61–79.

Kamariah, A. B. (2006). Malaysian smart school courseware: Lifelong learning tool for science, mathematics and IT teachers. *Malaysian Online Journal of Instructional Technology (MOJIT), 3*(2), 17–25.

Kamaruddin, N. (2010). Challenges of Malaysian developers in creating good interfaces for interactive courseware. *Turkish Online Journal of Educational Technology, 9*(1), 37–42.

Kaptelinin, V., & Nardi, B. A. (2006). *Acting with technology: Activity theory and interaction design*. MIT Press.

Kinzer, C., & Leu, D. J. (1997). Focus on research: The challenge of change: Exploring literacy and learning in electronic environments. *Language Arts*, *74*(2), 126–136.

Kirkwood, A. (2014). Teaching and learning with technology in higher education: Blended and distance education needs "joined-up thinking" rather than technological determinism. *Open Learning*, *29*(3), 206–221.

Kozlova, D. & Pikhart, M. (2021). The Use of ICT in Higher Education from the Perspective of the University Students, *Procedia Computer Science*, 192, 2309–2317.

Lee, M. J. W., McLoughlin, C., & Chan, A. (2008). Talk the talk: Learner-generated podcasts as catalysts for knowledge creation. *British Journal of Educational Technology*, *39*(3), 501–521.

Leontiev, A. M. (1974). *General Notion of Activity*. Moscow: Nauka

Lim, T. (2010). The use of Facebook for online discussions among distance students. *Turkish Online Journal of Distance Education*, *11*(4), 72–82.

Ling, S. E. Ariffin, S. R., Rahman, S., & Lai, K. L. (2010). Diversity in education using blended learning in Sarawak. *US-China Education Review*, *7*(2), 83–88.

Malaysian Examination Councils. (2006). *Malaysian University English test: Regulation test specifications, test format and sample questions*. Malaysian Examinations Council.

Maznah, R. (2004). eLearning in higher education institutions in Malaysia. *E-mentor*, *5*(7), 72–75.

MDC. (2005). The smart school roadmap 2005–2020: an educational odyssey – A consultative paper on the expansion of the smart school initiative to all schools in Malaysia: For multimedia development corporation (M. D. Corporation, Trans.). *Multimedia development corporation*. Kuala Lumpur: Ministry of Education Malaysia.

Melor, M. Y., & Rashidah, K. R. N. (2011). Motivation and attitude for learning English among year six students in primary rural school. *Procedia Social & Behavioral Sciences*, *15*(2011), 2631–2636.

Mirzajani, H., & Bayekolaei, M. D. (2016). Smart schools an innovation in education: Malaysia's experience. *Asian Journal of Education and Training*, *2*(1), 11–15.

Mohamed Amin Embi. (2011). e-Learning in Malaysian institutions of higher learning: Status, trends and challenges. *International lifelong learning conference (ICLLL 2011)*, Seri Pacific Hotel: Kuala Lumpur (14–15 November), 1–11.

Moser, F. Z. (2007). Faculty adoption of educational technology. *Educause Quarterly*, *30*(1), 66–69.

Motteram, G. (2013). *Innovations in learning technologies for English language teaching*. British Council.

Noble, D. F. (1998). Digital diploma mills: The automation of higher education. *Net-Worker*, *2*(2), 9–14.

Omar, A. H. (1992). *The linguistic scenery in Malaysia*. Dewan Bahasa dan Pustaka, Ministry of Education Malaysia.

Oxford, R., & Jung, S.-H. (2007). National guidelines for technology integration in TESOL programs: Factors affecting (non)implementation. In M. Peters, K. Murphy-Judy, R. Z. Lavine, & M. A. Kassen (Eds.), *Preparing and developing technology-proficient L2 teachers* (pp. 23–48). Computer Assisted Language Instruction Consortium.

Papacharissi, Z. A. (2010). *A networked self.* Routledge.

Prensky, M. (2001). Digital natives, digital immigrants Part 1. *On the Horizon, 9*(5), 1–6.

Rajaretnam, T. (2004). Using online grammar quizzes for language learning. *The Internet TESL Journal, X*(8) [Online]. Retrieved January 22, 2019, from http://iteslj.org/Articles/Rajaretnam-OnlineQuizzes.html

Roth, W.-M., & Lee, Y.-L. (2007). Vygotsky's neglected legacy: Cultural historical activity theory. *Review of Educational Research, 77*(2), 186–232.

Selvaraj, B. (2010). Curriculum reforms in Malaysia. *Voice of Academia, 5*(1), 51–60.

Selwyn, N. (2011). *Education and technology: Key issues and debates.* Continuum.

Siew-Eng, L., & Muuk, M. A. (2015). Blended learning in teaching secondary schools' English: A preparation for tertiary science education in Malaysia. *Procedia -Social and Behavioral Sciences, 167*(167), 293–300.

Singh, G. K. G., & Singh, S. K. G. (2008). Malaysian graduates' employability skills. *UniTAR e-Journal, 4*(1), 15–45.

Staker, H., & Horn, M. B. (2012). *Classifying K–12 blended learning.* Innosight Institute.

Thang, S. M., Mustaffa, R., Wong, F. F., Mohd. Noor, N., Mahmud, N., Latif, H., & Abd. Aziz, Mohd. S. (2013). A quantitative inquiry into the effects of blended learning on English language learning: The case of Malaysian undergraduates. *International Education Studies, 6*(6), 1.

Thang, S. M., Wong, F. F., Noor, N. M., Mustaffa, R., Mahmud, N., & Ismail, K. (2012). Using a blended approach to teach english for academic purposes: Malaysian students' perceptions of redesigned course materials. *International Journal of Pedagogies and Learning, 7*(2), 142–153.

Timmis, S., (2014). The dialectical potential of cultural historical activity theory for researching sustainable CSCL practices. *International Journal of Computer-Supported Collaborative Learning, 9*(1), 7–32.

Wai, C. C., & Seng, E. L. K. (2013). Measuring the effectiveness of blended learning environment: A case study in Malaysia. *Education and Information Technologies,* 1–15.

Zhao, Y. (2005). Technology and second language learning: Promises and problems. In *Technology in support of young second language students project.* Working Paper: Michigan State University, 1–31.

7 Lessons Learned from Navigating e-Campus UMK

Ramamurthy, Lena, Shafien, Syakirah, Azlan, Mohammad Affiq Kamarul and Mohd Nawi, Noor Syamimie

Introduction

The technology revolution has marked a significant phenomenon on the 21st century. Pen and pencil in class teaching and learning is no longer the sole practice in education. The dramatic expansion and extension of the use of technology especially in higher education has broadened the teaching and learning. This latest trend is now serving as an integral part of higher educational system. *Universiti Malaysia Kelantan* (UMK) particularly has applied e-Campus for years. This web-based learning system has gone through a long process to be fully accepted by the teachers and learners. Countless attempts have been made to introduce and implement the system to its users. This is especially harder for English language teaching and learning at first.

Digital technology has increasingly engaged remarkable public attention, and this has contributed to the formalisation of Internet use in teaching and learning. Studies have eminently encouraged the incorporation of the Internet in learning, and it is somehow deemed as necessary in the education environment today, be it through the social media, and/or learning applications via computer, smartphones or tablets. The current education system has to be tuned towards providing 21st-century skills needed by the learners for collaboration, creativity, critical thinking and communication; the thrusts of Education 4.0. In attaining the skills mentioned earlier, embracing online learning seems significant because it encourages the incorporation of those skills. For example, online learning encourages collaboration among learners through various collaborative learning applications available online. Learners can also use the online learning platform to sharpen their creativity and critical thinking skills through a more accessible myriad of reading materials and information. Finally, online learning irrefutably can enhance learners' communication skills through the use of communication devices such as smartphones and tablets in language lessons (Balula et al., 2015; Luo et al., 2015; Teodorescu, 2015; Wu, 2015).

DOI: 10.4324/9781003374190-7

With the vital impression given on the idea of online learning, teachers have to be one step ahead in mastering the techniques and principles of online learning to deliver effective lessons inside and outside the classrooms. Thus, UMK took the initiative by introducing a learning management system (LMS) to facilitate teaching and learning among teachers and learners. UMK has three campuses that cater for the three main field of studies. They are divided into Entrepreneurship and Business (Pengkalan Chepa Campus), Creative Technology and Heritage (Bachok Campus) and Agro-Based Industry and Earth Sciences (Jeli Campus). All these three campuses keep the system updated, syncing with current development in teaching and learning.

In this chapter, we aim to reflect our experiences in dealing with e-Campus, a Moodle-based LMS in UMK. We describe the origin of e-Campus UMK and link it to technology and English language teaching and learning. We also reflect on the advantages and disadvantages of the implementation of e-Campus as well as the initiatives taken by UMK in encouraging users to use the system. Lastly, future suggestions are recommended for further improvement and enhancement to the system.

The Origin of e-Campus UMK

e-Campus, according to Bele et al. (2014), is a web application designed for learning, learning management and multimedia learning content creation that can be accessed through various devices and platforms. e-Campus UMK is a Moodle based LMS used at UMK since 2016. Since its introduction, e-Campus has given a significant contribution towards enhancing teaching and learning in a number of aspects. e-Campus is the UMK version of a Moodle-based LMS, where just like many other academic institutions around the worlds, Moodle is used as an LMS platform for the purpose of teaching and learning. Since its first introduction at UMK, e-Campus is based on Moodle Version 2.0.

In many academic institutions, Moodle is used for blended learning, distance education, flipped classroom and other online-based assignments in schools, colleges and universities. The Moodle platform is customisable, and it can be tailored into private websites to serve the purpose of teaching and learning. At UMK, it is tailored into what is known as e-Campus. Before the Moodle platform is used as UMK LMS, UMK adopted a Universiti Pendidikan Sultan Idris (UPSI) based learning management platform known as MyGURU, or otherwise known as MyEdu at UMK.

Experience in Using e-Campus

Reflecting on our own experiences with e-Campus, we see several improvements in the process of teaching and learning; first being comprehensively paperless. Previously, before the introduction of the LMS in teaching and learning, plenty of papers had to be used to print teaching and learning materials for both teachers and learners. For instance, for a single class, teachers would need to print at least two sheets for each of their students. Considering the hundreds of teaching staff across all UMK campuses, this would result in a massive amount of wastage. On top of that, approximately 9,000 students would have to print out several assignments for their submissions every semester, adding to this issue. Fortunately, this situation has been reduced with the introduction of e-Campus. Now, teaching and learning materials no longer have to be printed out for classroom purposes, and learners can submit their assignments online. It is also worth noting that with the online submissions, there are no longer problems with finding learners' assessment sheets that may have gone missing. Instead, we can easily retrieve missing/hidden documents from the online system. The online system also allows us to see the learners' submission date and time automatically, so all late submissions can be noted.

As teachers, we are always concerned about learners' learning preparation prior to class. With e-Campus, it is now easier to provide learners with learning materials in the form of PowerPoint slides, PDF notes and lecture videos or audios before the start of class. Having these prepared, learners' access to these materials can be tracked, which allows teachers to know how many learners come to class prepared. The accessible feature within e-Campus has helped us to enhance the teaching and learning process. Finally, the introduction of e-Campus has also reduced our workload, for instance, using e-Campus' quiz application, all listening and grammar tests can now be done online and the system can automatically assess the answers and generate the marks. This saves hours of marking time and hence allows teachers to focus more on teaching and its preparation and become more creative in our classes. A lesson that is creatively crafted will produce creative learners that are independent. Quoting the words of Albert Einstein, 'it is the supreme art of the teacher to awaken joy in creative expression and knowledge'.

e-Campus Features

e-Campus UMK is now a robust and user-friendly system that offers ample of interactive features. This all-in-one platform serves as a platform to manage assessments and lessons. It promotes flexible learning and communication. Users can access e-Campus directly from https://ecampus.umk.edu.my. The system is linked to UMK Portal e-community. As shown in Figure 7.1, username and password are required for log-in purposes.

Once log-in is successful, users have to click on E-Learning (see Figure 7.2) and they will be led to the official page of e-Campus (see Figure 7.3).

On the dashboard, users can view other online users, calendar, courses, news and announcements, upcoming events and chatroom. This illustrates that there are a range of tools and features available on e-Campus. Teachers

Figure 7.1 Username and password are required

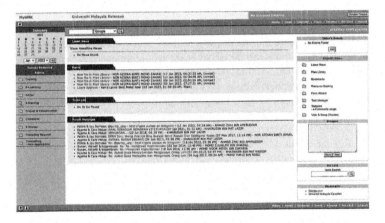

Figure 7.2 Click e-learning on the left side

use e-Campus to post announcement to learners, upload necessary handouts, and exercises (format in pdf, doc., txt and etc.). Useful slides, audios and videos from variety sources and formats (mp3, mp4, wav and etc.) can also be uploaded, whether that is directly to the platform or providing URL resources. Another breakthrough that e-Campus UMK has achieved is that it has integrated H5P into the system (see Figure 7.4). H5P is a free and open-source plugin that helps to deliver interactive HTML content on web platforms. This

Figure 7.3 Official UMK e-Campus dashboard

Figure 7.4 H5p

user-friendly plugin currently works with WordPress and Moodle. To the best of our knowledge, UMK is the first to use H5P in Malaysia.

We can also design our own quizzes using e-Campus. The Quiz activity enables us to create quizzes with various types of questions, like matching, short-answer, and multiple choice which can be utilised in English language reading and listening practice. For English language writing, we typically utilise Wiki and Turnitin Assignment 2. Wiki is helpful especially when learners are doing pair or group assignments. We found this activity is meaningful to learners as they can work together and learn from each other by viewing and editing each other's work. Such collaborative writing and peer review activities are often being stressed in teaching and learning English language. For Turnitin Assignment 2, it links assignments to Turnitin (see Figure 7.5),

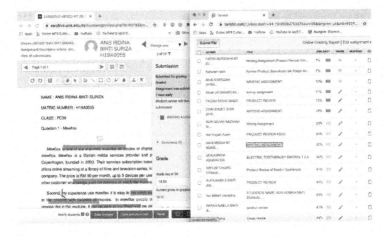

Figure 7.5 Turnitin assignment 2

an application that enables teachers to assess and trace the originality of the learners' work and provide firsthand feedback for learners' written work.

It is even more interactive when conducting lessons online using a feature called BigBlueButtonBN. Lecturing is no longer restricted to time and space as it is possible to conduct a real-time class using this open-source web conferencing system for distance learning. Besides, forums and chatrooms are often utilised for learners to share ideas and knowledge. What makes all these activities so significant is that Blended Learning is now officially implemented not just in UMK, but also other educational institutions. This means that during lectures, teachers can use the activities mentioned previously to integrate technology into learning. We conduct our online lecture by asking questions in the forum or Chatroom and also lecturing through real-time conference using the BigBlueButtonBN feature (see Figure 7.6). Teaching and learning English language are different from other content-based subjects such that often, learners can learn on their own without teachers. Learners have no excuse in attending the online lecture, forums and chatrooms because it is accessible anywhere and anytime. This is handier when the learners' attendance can be monitored using the Attendance feature on e-Campus.

There are also some exclusive games on e-Campus, namely Book with questions, Crossword, Cryptex, Hangman and Hidden Picture. Games like Crossword (see Figure 7.7) and Hangman are good for vocabulary enhancement. These two games can be auto-generated by using words from either a Glossary (another advantageous activity for English language vocabulary enhancement) or quizzes (that we have designed). Learning new vocabulary

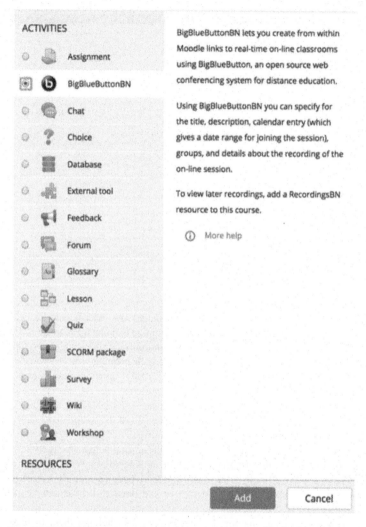

Figure 7.6 BigBlueButtonBN

is not an easy process. Various drilling activities are needed to help learners in memorising and applying the vocabulary in spoken and written communication. Doing such activities can help learners to cope and tackle daunting fossilised errors. Besides, these activities can also aid learners who enrol in

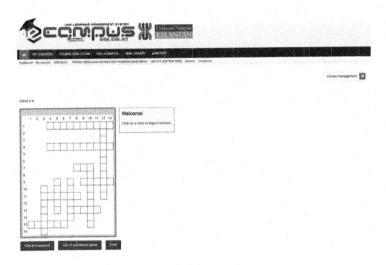

Figure 7.7 Exclusive game (crossword)

English for Specific Purpose courses like English for Science and English for Business Communication. These two subjects are rather new to learners. Therefore, we use these games to help encourage and engage learners to the environment and aid them in faster acculturation. This allows them to reflect on what they have learned, thus accelerating their learning.

The recent 'Alternative e-Assessment Gala Day' has even announced that e-Campus UMK is developing to link more items with e-Campus. One of them is Instagram (IG). English language teachers at UMK are anticipating this as we are currently using Instagram for one of the assignments (Insta-entry) enlisted in the Advanced Grammar course.

Overall, UMK e-Campus is now playing a vital role and largely integrated in our English language teaching and learning. With the use of e-Campus UMK, English language teaching and learning is becoming more time efficient, effective, interactive and impactful. Researchers like Nomass (2013) stressed that English as second language (ESL) learners need other language support like technologies in helping them to learn English language. Barrett and Liu (2016) further asserted that Malaysian teachers have to incorporate technology in teaching English language. Therefore, e-Campus UMK serves as one of the best choices to be integrated in ESL teaching and learning.

Other examples of features that we use on e-Campus are YouTube (Figure 7.8) and Online assignment (Figure 7.9):

Lecture Video - Understanding the Main Idea

Figure 7.8 Embedded YouTube video

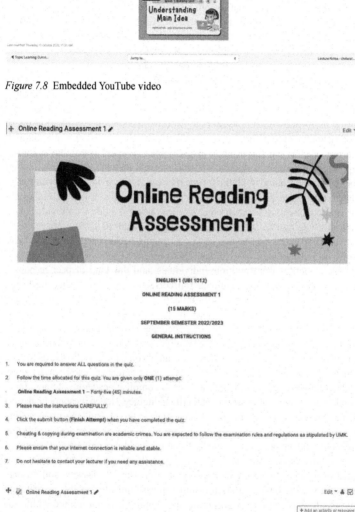

Figure 7.9 Online assignment

The Advantages of e-Campus UMK

As we explored the e-Campus LMS, we came to an understanding that the incorporation of technology in the teaching of English as a second language could be significant. There are various research studies carried out that focus on the potential of technology in boosting learners' mastery in language. Through e-Campus, what Ybarra and Green (2003) suggested has been found to be true, in particular that e-Campus serves as a fundamental platform in providing UMK ESL learners with meaningful language experiences as they can learn English through the incorporation of e-Campus. This is because their learning is not always limited to the classroom sessions, but notes and practices can always be accessed beyond the classroom walls.

Similarly, it has also been found that the teaching and learning process that we had experienced through e-Campus matched to what many researchers had proposed, such that the use of online learning tools create a helpful and reassuring atmosphere for the learners to improve their writing skills in terms of quality and quantity (Yunus et al., 2013). In our classes, for example, through the use of chat and forum apps on e-Campus, learners were enthusiastic in replying to comments online as it mimicked what they did everyday with their social media accounts. With the forum application too, speaking activities were better encouraged among learners as they posted videos of themselves speaking and commenting on each other's videos using a guide we provided. This kind of vlogging-like activity is what Kelly and Safford (2009) referred to as encouraging interaction in language classrooms because it serves as a 'real-world digital medium'. As Holder (2006) asserted, online blogs let bloggers receive responses from multiple individuals, and this kind of peer responses is more efficient than conventional self-correction. We found that the forum activity on e-Campus, through a forum app, could be set in a blog-like format. As Lenhart et al. (2008) emphasised, blogs are common platforms for youths to express their opinions, and there is adequate indication to say that learners with personal blogs are likely to be creative writers in colleges. Thus, through e-Campus, we believe language learners can become more well-read as Kasper (2000) mentioned in LaCava (2002), as second language learners who study with technology are multiliterate as they accomplish academic literacy, functional literacy, electronic literacy and critical literacy. Hence it cannot be denied that technology can certainly be advantageous in the second language teaching and learning, and e-Campus can therefore be described as an instrument that caters for all language skills, namely listening, speaking, reading and writing.

We have also learnt that with e-Campus, language lessons can be managed in a more organised way as we can pre-plan the lessons and arrange them on weekly basis. Through forum and assignment plug-ins, learners are allowed to work with their group members, and this is not limited within the classroom walls. Learners can participate in the learning activity even though they are not physically sitting together in groups. One of the situations that we think is relevant to share is when learners encountered problems with meeting their group members for a discussion. This usually occurred during the monsoon season, when some of the learners could not leave their hometown after school breaks due to flooding. With e-Campus, this was no longer an issue for the learners as they could meet online. To prepare a video presentation, all of them could make recordings separately, then combine them online and submit it as a group presentation through e-Campus. This has also made it easier for teachers as there was no need to schedule face-to-face presentation sessions, leaving more time to focus on other tasks.

e-Campus has also been used in blended learning. Albiladi and Alshareef (2019) highlighted that blended learning can provide opportunities for learners to practice the language beyond the class settings. We found this true in UMK as quizzes could be set via the quiz plug-in available on e-Campus. Our experience tells us that one semester is usually inadequate to cover all the syllabus due to the many public holidays in Malaysia, which means that many classes are cancelled. However, through the quiz plug-in, we can create practice exercises in advance and let the learners do the practices during holidays. The good thing about this is we can always monitor students' progress through the quizzes that they have attempted. The system would automatically mark the answers set in advance and give instant feedback to learners; something that is rather impossible for a teacher to do in a class of 20–30 learners. This reflects what a language learning beyond classroom settings is.

Limitations in Using e-Campus

Regardless of the proved findings and empirical studies on the advantages of integrating technology into teaching and learning, in reality, we still have to face certain limitations and challenges. The following are some of the challenges we identified in our reflections:

Accessibility

When e-Campus was first introduced, the biggest challenge we had was with the server. Very often, using the system was time-consuming because of the time it took to load the page that we were looking for. Lessons were almost always interrupted due to slow connection. Technical faults like internet disruption and restricted internet access were other obstacles that we often encountered during our lessons. Certain areas in UMK as well as learners' accommodations also had issues with the Internet access points.

Features Are Not User-Friendly

There were some weaknesses in the features and design. For example, Wiki was rather complicated to some teachers and learners. ESL teachers had to 'sacrifice' their lesson time by explaining and teaching learners the technical aspects of the system when they were supposed to focus on teaching English language. As a result, teachers suffered the loss of time in delivering their lessons. Both teachers and learners took time to digest and explore the feature and system. When creating a language test, teachers often had to redesign the pattern of the questions because the design feature on e-Campus is limited. The process was very much frustrating and tedious.

Lack of Exposure in Using the Platform

Learners had little to no idea how to access the materials and how to upload their assignments. Apart from that, insufficient training and lack of pedagogical programmes and technical learning among learners and teachers were some of the reasons e-Campus became a challenge to them.

Lack of Awareness among the Academics

Negative attitudes towards the use of technology in teaching and learning among the academics gave a significant impact on the incorporation of e-Campus in teaching and learning English language. Some teachers were scared of and refused to be open about the integration of e-Campus in teaching and learning. This was especially true in ESL teaching and learning in which teachers still preferred face-to-face lessons and activities. They did not see the benefits technology could bring to their learners.

Facilities/Infrastructure

Lack of facilities was also another issue. Limited computer labs across the campus made teaching and learning harder for both learners and teachers. Moreover, the existing computers were outdated and computers required maintenance. Latest teaching tools and activities could not be utilised during teaching and learning activities because the system failed to work. In addition, when classes were conducted in a computer lab, we were often left without any technical support or assistance from the technician.

Initiatives Taken by UMK

Realising the limitations in using e-Campus, many initiatives have been taken by the university. Such initiatives include:

Organise Workshop/Training by Stages

Workshops on e-Campus and e-learning is conducted from time to time. Representatives from each faculty and centre are trained beforehand so that they can conduct a hands-on workshop and training to the other staff in their respective faculty or centre.

Provide YouTube Tutorials

YouTube tutorials are also provided for further revision and for those who have missed the workshop. Clear step-by-step instructions are thoroughly explained in the video.

Provide a Manual

Manuals are provided online and are downloadable too. It provides a step-by-step instruction to learners and teachers.

Improve the System and Server

The server has been improved. It can now take a larger size of uploaded files and no more disruptions in between. The uploading process is much quicker than before.

Upgrade the Internet Coverage

Knowing the Internet coverage can be limited, the university took initiative to upgrade the service in all campuses as well as in learners' accommodations.

Create New Regulations

Since the Ministry of Education Malaysia has announced that *Blended Learning* should be integrated in education, the university has made it a compulsory requirement in the e-LNPT (*e-Laporan Nilaian Prestasi Tahunan*), which refers to the performance appraisal of the staff. This is to encourage the incorporation of e-Campus among academics in their teaching and learning activities. The system is also closely monitored by the university and every semester each faculty/centre receives a set of analyses which lists Top Achievers on different levels: faculty level, course level and individual level.

Create Awareness

To inspire and encourage the academics to be aware of and use e-Campus, recognition and awards are given to the top achievers. The most recent one would be the Alternative e-Assessment Gala Day organised by the Centre of Excellence & Academic Development, UMK on 21st January 2020. Best Practices e-Assessment Award and Best Practitioner e Assessment Award by individual and course level have been awarded to the top achievers. These top achievers will be sent to participate in an Innovation Competition at university levels and also international levels. Besides, those who achieve the requirements of Blended Learning also receive a Certificate of Blended Learning Achievement.

Upgrade the System

A range of features have been added and embedded over time. As previously mentioned, the latest feature is H5P and the next is IG plug-ins. This is considered as one of the breakthroughs made by the university in linking social media to e-Campus for teaching and learning.

Conclusion

It is undeniable that technology is a trend that can shape the future. Universities and institutions like UMK have put a lot of effort to pave the way for creating and enhancing a stronger education system for the future generation. It is believed that ESL teaching and learning when fused with technology can help to create a favourable learning environment to learners. Despite some limitations, we believe that e-Campus is still an effective platform for ESL teaching and learning.

References

Albiladi, W. S., & Alshareef, K. K. (2019). Blended learning in English teaching and learning: A review of the current literature. *Journal of Language Teaching and Research, 10*(2), 232–238. http://doi.org/10.17507/jltr.1002.03

Balula, A., Marques, F., & Martins, C. (2015). Bet on top hat – challenges to improve language proficiency. In *Proceedings of EDULEARN15 conference 6–8 July 2015* (pp. 2627–2633). Barcelona.

Bele, J. L., Bele, D., Hauptman, S., Kozuh, I., & Debevc, M. (2014). eCampus as a platform for ubiquitous learning. *Proceedings of the 2014 IEEE global engineering education conference (EDUCON)*, 1–7. Institute Electrics and Electronics Engineers (IEEE). https://doi.org/10.1109/EDUCON.2014.7130486

Barrett, Neil & Liu, Gi-Zen. (2016). Global Trends and Research Aims for English Academic Oral Presentations: Changes, Challenges, and Opportunities for Learning Technology. *Review of Educational Research.* 86, 1227–1271. 10.3102/00346543 16628296.

Holder, C. R. (2006, January 1). *New media and new literacies: Perspectives on change.* https://er.educause.edu/articles/2006/1/new-media-and-new-literacies-perspectives-on-change

Kasper, L. F. (2000). New technologies, new literacies: Focus discipline research and ESL learning communities. *Language Learning & Technology, 4*(2), 105–128.

Kelly, A., & Safford, K. (2009). Does teaching complex sentences have to be complicated? Lessons from children's online writing. *Literacy, 43*(3), 118–122. https://doi.org/10.1111/j.1741-4369.2009.00501.x

LaCava, D. S. (2002). *Perspective transformation in adult ESL learners using internet technology* (Publication No. 3056144) [Doctoral dissertation, Fordham University] ProQuest Dissertations & Theses Global.

Lenhart, A., Arafeh, S., Smith, A., & Macgill, A. R. (2008, April 24). *Writing, technology and teens.* Pew Research Centre. www.pewinternet.org/

Luo, B. R., Lin, Y. L., Chen, N. S., & Fang, W. C. (2015). Using mobile device to facilitate English communication and willingness to communicate in a communicate language teaching classroom. *Proceedings of the 15th International conference on advanced learning technologies* (pp. 320–322). IEEE.

Nomass, B. B. (2013). The impact of using technology in teaching English as a second language. *English Language and Literature Studies, 3*(1), 111–116. https://doi.org/10.5539/ells.v3n1p111

Teodorescu, A. (2015). Mobile learning and its impact on business English learning. *Procedia – Social and Behavioral Sciences, 180,* 1535–1540.

Wu, Q. (2015). Pulling mobile assisted language learning (MALL) into the mainstream: MALL in broad practice. *PLoS ONE, 10*(5), e0128762.

Ybarra, R., & Green, T. (2003). Using technology to help ESL/EFL learners develop language skills. *The Internet TESL Journal, 9*(3). http://iteslj.org/Articles/Ybarra-Technology.html

Yunus, M. M., Nordin, N., Salehi, H., Choo, H. S., & Embi, M. A. (2013). Pros and Cons of Using ICT in Teaching ESL Reading and Writing. *International Education Studies, 6*(7), 119–130.

Index

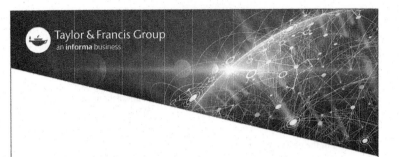